Crib Notes for

THE
FIRST YEAR
OF
MARRIAGE

Crib Notes for

THE
FIRST YEAR
OF
MARRIAGE

A Survival Guide for Newlyweds

EVERETT DE MORIER

Fairview Press
Minneapolis

Published by Fairview Press, 2450 Riverside Avenue South, Minneapolis, MN 55454.

Library of Congress Cataloging-in-Publication Data
De Morier, Everett, 1962—
        Crib notes for the first year of marriage / Everett De Morier.
            p.   cm.
        ISBN 1-57749-030-4 (alk. paper)
            1. Marriage—Handbooks, manuals, etc.   2. Married people—Finance,
        Personal—Handbooks, manuals, etc.   I. Title
        HQ734.D385   1997
        306.81—dc21   97–7772

First Printing: May 1997
Printed in the United States of America
01 00 99 98 97   7 6 5 4 3 2 1

Cover design: Rich Rossiter

Publisher's Note: The publications of Fairview Press, including *Crib Notes for the First Year of Marriage*, do not necessarily reflect the philosophy of Fairview Health System or its treatment programs.

For a free catalogue, call toll-free 1–800–544–8207.

To my best friend, Debbie-Jean—
because if she never married me,
this would be a book about fishing.

TABLE OF CONTENTS

INTRODUCTION

I t happens. The right person, the right time, the right feeling, and pow! You've found that special someone, the person with whom you want to spend the rest of your life.

Then comes the wedding, or more specifically, the agonizing process of planning the wedding. Opinions and advice flow freely from the consultants and planners—and from friends, parents, grandparents, aunts and uncles, future in-laws, co-workers, caterers, seamstresses, tailors, musicians, bartenders, stationery designers, napkin and matchbook manufacturers, lighting specialists, postmasters, and the friendly cashier at the grocery store. The list of contributors is endless, as are the minutia to be decided upon.

But all the planning and fine-tuning are well worth the $1.89 for the bottle of aspirin required to get through the process, for they ensure that your special day will be perfect. Besides, it will all be over so quickly, and then you'll be back to living your normal life.

Or so you think.

Suddenly, the wedding is over, and things aren't normal at all. You have myriad things to do—change your name on your driver's license (if you have taken your spouse's name), add your spouse's name to your bank account(s) and your insurance forms, clean and preserve the wedding gown, find spots for all the lovely punch bowls you received as wedding gifts, write all those thank-you cards, and so on. Plus, it seems your blessed event got you registered on some sort of national list for telemarketers, because all of a sudden salespeople are calling nightly, selling everything from storm windows to magazine subscriptions.

There's enough stuff to fill two months' worth of "to do" lists, but thankfully, the "to do's" are mostly straightforward. Nothing is too complicated or confused at this point in your life together. True complication and confusion come later. For instance, how can a newly married couple save on car insurance and company benefit packages? What is the best strategy for filing income taxes as a couple for the first time? What pitfalls can be avoided when you move in together for the first time (assuming you did not live together before the wedding)? How do you set up a budget? How do you learn to communicate with each other? (It will change, believe me.) How much should you be saving for the future? And what about your first fight?

Unfortunately, newlyweds are rarely told about such weighty topics, probably because most people view them as too somber or boring to mix with the lighter, happier topics of falling in love and planning a wedding. Besides, don't people figure it out for themselves eventually, anyway? Millions of couples get married each year, and they make it through the first year of marriage successfully. They have since the beginning of time.

That's true, certainly. But the transition from thinking and acting as a single person to thinking and acting as a couple, without losing your identity in the process, can be difficult. Indeed, in the first year of marriage each spouse inherits an entirely new family and circle of friends, and must learn to deal with the pressures and expectations of these various relationships. It is during the first year that issues about personal space are negotiated, when habits and lifestyle must be compromised. And it is during the first year that couples establish the routines and set the future course of the marriage itself.

I BEGAN TEACHING my workshop "From Engagement through the First Year of Marriage" for two reasons: the first was simply to get in front of a crowd; the second, less egotistical, reason was to share what I'd learned during my own first year of marriage. During that year, my wife and I did a lot of things the hard way. We worked harder, took more time, and spent more money than we really had to. If we knew then what we know now, our first year would have been different.

Not that the first year must go smoothly if the marriage is to be successful in the long run. But it is unproductive and even hurtful to expend resources on simple, silly things when there are so many legitimately significant issues to deal with during the first year of marriage. The goal of this book, then, is to save newly married couples time, frustration, and money.

That money is a consistent theme throughout the book is no accident. Money is often the single most explosive issue during the first year of marriage. In fact, couples who have attended my workshops have wanted to know more about money—how to save it, invest it, and avoid fighting about it—than any other topic. Like it or not, the financial picture changes in the first year of marriage. Slowly, slowly, slowly, your financial viewpoint melds with that of your spouse, until one morning your mind's eye squints to remember those days of living off ramen noodles and macaroni and cheese.

CRIB NOTES FOR THE FIRST YEAR OF MARRIAGE is the first book for newlyweds designed by newlyweds. Guided by the questions, needs, and concerns of the participants in my marriage workshops, I have collected and organized a large body of materials and ideas that newly married couples should find useful, even indispensable. This book is the result. Information that was previously unavailable in a single resource has now been compiled in this book.

It was fun writing Crib Notes. Now in our fifth year of marriage, with a two-year-old child who will forever more remind us how long we've been married, my wife and I found it interesting to review our first year of marriage in preparation for writing this book. Sometimes it seemed like several lifetimes ago, and other times it seemed like only yesterday.

The mistakes we made that year were small in the great scheme of things: we spent more money than we had to; we fought more than we had to; and we wasted time sweating the small things while struggling to find time for the important ones. If we'd known then what we know now, we would have fought less, avoided debt, and had more fun. This book is about teaching you what you need to know in your first year of marriage to fight less, avoid debt, and have more fun. At least, that is my wish for you. Good luck!

THE POST-WEDDING WEDDING GUIDE

'The time has come' the Walrus said,
  'To talk of many things:
Of shoes—and ships—and sealing-wax—
  Of cabbages—and kings—
And why the sea is boiling hot—
And whether pigs have wings.'
          —*Lewis Carroll*, Through the Looking Glass

It's very simple. People meet. They fall in love. They get married. She agrees to love and cherish him. To remember all the birthdays and anniversaries of everyone in his family. To support him through at least three get-rich-quick schemes, at least one of which involves owning a sports bar. And to allow him to use the phrase "getting back in shape," implying that he once was.

He agrees to love, honor, and obey her. To supply at least three major credit cards and one major department store card. To learn to roll the toilet paper over the spool rather than under it, and to sit and cuddle with her while watching *The Bridges of Madison County* and *Steel Magnolias*, making no sarcastic or disgruntled noises in the background.

Then begins the being married stuff. To be sure, the first year of marriage is a time of change, adaptation, negotiation, compromise, and lots more that we'll get into in the rest of the book. But no time in marriage is as crazy as the first month. Ask anybody. The first month is not as insane as the time spent planning and preparing for the wedding, of course—that is in its own special category of crazy—but the wedding takes place *before* the marriage, so it doesn't count.

Throughout this book, the subtleties of marriage, especially the first year of marriage, will be discussed: methods of saving money, interacting with in-laws, avoiding and getting out of debt. This chapter, however, is designed simply to help you relax and quickly complete the activities associated with the first month of marriage. Opening a joint bank account, for example. Or picking up the wedding photos. Writing thank-you cards. Buying a new sofa. And so on.

Such activities fall into two simple categories: things to do and things to buy.

Things to Do

BELOW IS A LIST of those things most couples do in their first month of marriage. This list is not meant to be exhaustive; nor will each item apply to every couple. The list is merely provided as a reference or a reminder to help ease your transition into married life.

1. Changing your personal identification and account information. Traditionally, wives have taken their husband's last name, but that is not always the case today. For example, some women are keeping their maiden names; others are taking their husband's name but keeping their own and hyphenating the two. Some are hyphenating their maiden and married names, and their husbands are doing the same.

For those individuals who change their name after marriage, and about 60 percent do, it may seem like notifying all the necessary people would best be accomplished by taking out a full-page ad in the newspaper. In reality, there are only a handful of changes you need to make right away:

- **Bank account.** Because banks are state-regulated, policies on account changes will vary from state to state, and, for that matter, from bank to bank. Contact your bank shortly after your wedding and follow the necessary procedures. Better yet, call your bank ahead of time and find out what paperwork and identification are required. Contrary to the reputation for endless red tape many banks have earned, the procedure usually takes only a few minutes and is simple and straightforward, often requiring only a marriage license or some another common form of identification. You may even get a free cup of coffee and a donut for your trouble.

- **Driver's license.** Though it may seem like informing the state of your marital status is "Big Brotherism," notifying your state department of motor vehicles of name and address changes should be a priority. Important information is sent to the address on your license—for example, license tabs and voter registration. Besides, you didn't really think you were going to get out of paying those parking tickets, did you?

- **Insurance policies.** When you contact your insurance agent (provided you use the same agent for both your car insurance and homeowner's/renter's insurance), find out how much it would cost to insure both you and your spouse, and your car(s), on the same policy. Typically, putting both of you on the same policy will save you around 30 percent—in addition to the amount you're already saving by being the responsible married driver you are. Having one joint policy also simplifies your life when it comes to paying bills.

  It usually costs an additional 40 percent of the premium to add a spouse to an existing health insurance policy. Look at both your policies (assuming you both have health insurance) and select the one with the best coverage for the lowest cost—comprehensive coverage, ease of use, lowest out-of-pocket costs for deductible, prescriptions, co-pays, and so forth. Having a joint health insurance policy can save hundreds of dollars a year—60 percent or more of the premium for the second spouse—and ensures that you both receive the best medical care available to you.

  If neither you nor your spouse have health insurance, you may want to consider private medical insurance. It will be expensive, but you may be able to lower the cost by getting a family rate for the two of you. Consider, too, getting major medical insurance, which will cover emergency hospital stays and accidents.

- **Income tax and investment information.** As a married person, you have two choices for your tax status on your W-4 form: married and filing jointly, or married but filing separately. If you file jointly you will be taxed at a lower rate, which means less money will be taken out of each paycheck. However, your refund at the end of the year will be lower, or you may owe money. If you file separately you'll be taxed at a higher rate, which means more taxes will be taken out of your paycheck, but you may receive a larger return. (Consider that a large income tax return means that you've been making an interest-free loan to the government.)

You'll also want to name your new spouse as the beneficiary of any company life insurance policies, or pension or 401(k) plans. If you have a personnel or human resources department at your place of employment, you'll be able to change your tax status, address, insurance forms, bank account for direct deposit, and so forth, at the same time.

If unemployed, you'll want to contact your local office of unemployment benefits. Most require a social security card, or proof of social security number, and a marriage certificate to change your name, as well as proof of new address to change your address.

- **Social Security card.** If you change your name, you will have to get a new social security card. You keep the same social security number, but your name change is registered with the government. The process is very simple. All you need to do is go to your nearest social security office or call the Social Security Administration (800) 772-1213 and request a name-change form.

- **School information.** If you are a full-time student, you will need to contact the registrar's office to notify the college of your change in marital status. Scholarship and other financial aid files, housing requirements and procedures, and other general school policies may be affected. Most schools require married students to fill out a form and bring in their marriage license, but some will accept a newspaper clipping as proof.

- **Credit cards and subscriptions.** The easiest way to change your name on a credit card is to fill out the portion on the bill that asks for changes and send it in with your next payment. If you are adding your spouse to the account, most credit card companies require you to request additional cards in writing. You can take care of magazine subscriptions and catalogs as they come up for renewal.

- **Post office.** Assuming you will be living together after the wedding, and assuming one of you will have to move to accomplish that living arrangement, the simplest way to continue receiving all your mail at your new address is to fill out a change of address form at the post office. But then you will receive not only the mail you want but the mail you don't want—catalogs, solicitations, junk mail. I recommend not bothering with the post office, because by alerting the sources of important information you will already be getting what you need to get. Besides, there's no better way to weed out those pesky Victoria's Secret catalogs.

2. Opening a joint bank account. There is one advantage to opening a joint checking account: it costs less to maintain one account than two. Many financial groups recommend that couples have a joint checking account to simplify organization and record keeping. Moreover, many psychologists recommend the practice as an opportunity to deal with a controlling nature, a chance to practice trusting your spouse and thinking in terms of "our" money rather than "yours" and "mine."

Of course, it is up to you. My parents were happily married for thirty-five years with two separate checking accounts.

3. Writing the thank-you cards. Though it is one of the easiest things to do, getting those thank-you cards written and mailed is the single most procrastinated chore after getting married. So much so that a six-month rule evolved to ease the burden newlyweds feel about completing this arduous task. Of course, to a guest who doesn't receive a thank-you note within five months of selecting, purchasing, wrapping, and transporting a lovely heartfelt gift to you and your new mate, even two months may be pushing it.

The best advice: Keep the cards simple and get them done as quickly as possible. A simple, informal alternative to the traditional thank-you card is a postcard made from one of your honeymoon pictures—a fun shot of the two of you clowning around, or a romantic pose in the sunset, perhaps. Whatever the scene, friends and family will enjoy a visual memento of the love you and your spouse share as much as, if not more than, a thank-you card, regardless of how fine the card is (let's face it, most stationery looks the same) or how well it matches the color scheme of your wedding. And the best part of a postcard: there's less writing space to fill.

Another trick is to prioritize the order in which you send the cards—say, grandparents first, then aunts and uncles and other relatives, then friends, then co-workers and associates, then parents (don't forget the people who shelled out all that money). Assigning an order is a useful way of dividing and organizing the task into manageable chunks, and it assures that cranky Aunt Edna will get her thank-you note in a timely fashion.

The easiest way to get thank-you notes done is to write a few each night, while you're talking about your hectic days at work or watching TV, for example. This should be a joint effort. Make it a part of your nightly routine and each do five or six cards. That way, even if you had 200 guests at your wedding, it will take less than three weeks to work through the list. And it's more fun than spending a frustrating Sunday afternoon at the kitchen table in a thank-you card marathon from hell, trying to get them all in Monday's mail.

4. Ordering wedding photographs. Ah, the photographs. Scenes from your wedding day that will forever remind you that your hair was sticking up and that the best man had his corsage on crooked. Everyone involved will want to see the pictures as soon as possible after the wedding and, more than likely, will want every good shot the photographer snapped. Unfortunately, prints, especially in larger, frameable sizes, can get expensive quickly. Usually the photographer's fee covers only his or her time at the wedding and the production of proofs. Prints are an additional expense and, depending on the number and sizes needed, are usually much more than the initial fee.

If possible, try to buy the negatives from the photographer for one set price, either when you set up the contract for shooting your wedding or when you're ready to order prints. You'll spend a fraction of what the photographer would charge, and you can have as many reprints made as you want, even years later. Make no mistake, someone will want a photo of the wedding party two years afterwards. Some photographers prefer to sell the negatives because it saves them time and they can go on to the next job. Others won't because the money they make off the reprints is the bulk of their income.

5. Preserving the wedding gown. If you had a traditional wedding with a formal wedding gown, and are not planning to sell the gown, you'll probably want to preserve it. Many dry cleaners offer this service, which includes cleaning and packing the dress in an airtight box, with a plastic liner for viewing, so it won't yellow or age. Once packed, it should remain in that condition for years, ready to hand down to the next generation.

The cost is usually $100–$150. The time it takes to clean and preserve the gown usually depends on the season. In the spring and early summer, when weddings are more common, it can take up to three months to get the gown back.

To save yourself a possible nervous breakdown, examine your gown at the cleaners when you go to pick it up. Although such a mistake is rare, it is possible to mix up wedding gowns. And because the gown is packed away and may not be opened for years, the mistake can go unnoticed for years. If by looking through the plastic you're uncertain the gown you have is yours, take the dress out. It's better to break the seal now than to find out twenty years later you've been safeguarding the wrong dress.

First Month (Or So) To-Do List
• **Change name (if applicable) and address on important accounts and documents**
>   **Company personnel records**
>   **School**
>   **Social security card**
>   **Driver's license**
>   **Credit cards**
>   **Post office (if you want all mail forwarded)**
• **Add spouse to personal accounts**
>   **Bank**
>   **—Open joint bank account**
>   **Personal investments**
>   **—IRAs**
>   **—Mutual funds**
>   **—Stocks**
>   **—Treasury bonds**
>   **School emergency notification**
• **Add spouse to company records**
>   **Change tax status**

Change direct deposit to joint accounts
Company investment and retirement plans
 —401(k)
 —Life insurance
 —Investments
Company insurance and other benefit plans
 —Get quote for one health plan to cover both you
  and your spouse
 —Get quote for one car insurance plan
 —Get quote for one life insurance plan
- Send out thank-you cards
- Get wedding photographs
- Preserve wedding gown

Things to Buy

NOW COMES the fun part: spending the money. You may have spent all the dollar dance money on your honeymoon—that's fine, that money is meant to have fun with anyway—but you still have a pile of cash burning a hole in your joint account pocket. Some you received as wedding gifts; some was refunded when you returned the matching chartreuse towel set and those four extra blenders you received.

Every young couple starting out needs certain things. But while you may be tempted to spend every cent you have on those designer gadgets that look great but you'll never use—pasta makers, milk-shake blenders, and waffle irons, to name a few—don't go hog-wild. More than likely, the pang of urgent desire you're feeling is little more than a fleeting fancy. It will go away within hours of leaving the store. Instead, make a list of the things you think you need, then prioritize that list according to urgency and importance. As you calculate what you can afford, concentrate on the top items on your list.

For big-ticket items, such as a house or cabin, a savings plan will probably be in order (budgeting is discussed in a later chapter). Rather than leaving that money in a savings account, however, where you're earning only 2 or 3 percent interest and the money is readily accessible for "emergency purchases," try investing. Make your money work for you while you're working so hard to save it. A five-year CD,

for example, or a mutual fund or savings bonds will earn more interest than a savings account, and will increase your savings more quickly. Plus, early withdrawal penalties will deter those periodic urges to
borrow from it (investing strategies will be covered later in the book).
Consult an investment professional or financial planner to select the
right savings and investment plan for you.

While you're saving for your dream house, however, you'll probably have to purchase less expensive items, like furniture and appliances, to set up your home. When shopping for such items, keep in
mind that every dollar you spend now is a dollar you won't have to
spend later. With that in mind, below is a list of money-saving ideas
and some ways to get the most for your wedding-gift dollars on specific purchases. The golden rule: anything over $10 is worth shop-
ping around for.

- **Furniture.** Shop for furniture at a furniture specialty store rather
  than a department store. The furniture is usually of better quality, and furniture stores tend to offer better service, including free
  delivery. The furniture industry has two big sales a year, one in
  February and the other in early summer, and you can't go wrong
  around the first of the year. Most stores have great sales in
  January to get rid of excess Christmas stock. Never buy new furniture that's not on sale.

  Another option is estate and moving sales. Many wonderful
  bargains can be found by settling for slightly, or gently, used furniture. Antiques are sometimes a good investment as well. Garage
  sales generally offer lower-quality merchandise, particularly when
  it comes to furniture.

- **TVs, VCRs, and stereos.** The rule here is, watch weekly ads and
  flyers, and be patient. This industry is very competitive. More
  than likely, if you act too early you'll see the same TV for $50 less
  a month later. Stores that sell stereos tend to cater to the school
  crowd and usually have big sales in September and January. Shop
  at the chain superstores, many of which offer to match or beat the
  price of any competitor. Read *Consumer Reports* to find out which
  models are the best value—that is, which are of the highest quality and require the fewest repairs for the cost.

- **Computers.** This industry, too, is extremely competitive. But cost is not the only consideration when it comes to purchasing computer equipment. Technology is changing so rapidly that what was state-of-the-art yesterday is obsolete today. When selecting a system, choose one that will satisfy your needs in the short term and can be upgraded in the future.

The single most important choice in buying a computer system is the software that drives it—Windows or Macintosh. More than 80 percent of all software sold is Windows-based. Macintosh versions of popular programs are usually available, but are often more expensive than Windows versions. You can always upgrade hardware, but once you've decided on the platform you'll need to stick with it, or buy a whole new system later. The exception to this is Macintosh, which several years ago came out with systems that can run both the Macintosh operating system and DOS.

The platform you choose will depend largely on what you'll be using your computer for. If you plan on banking electronically or organizing your finances with your computer, there are excellent software packages available, in both Windows and Macintosh, that can help you do everything from creating and tracking a budget to preparing your taxes. If you'll be using your computer for work you bring home, you'll want a system that is compatible with your employer's (keeping in mind, of course, that typical Generation X-ers will change jobs at least seven times throughout their careers). And if you work at home, you'll want a system that is compatible with those used in the industry in which you work. Most businesses use Windows applications, while desktop publishing and design industries prefer Macintosh.

If you've already started looking for a computer system you've probably heard or seen examples of multimedia systems, which require sound and video cards and CD-ROM drives. If you're planning to join the world of multimedia, whether to play computer games, edit videos, or design interactive Web pages, it's better to buy your system preassembled as a multimedia unit. Upgrading is possible but complicated and expensive, with kits running from $300 to $500. Most software packages come on CDs now, so it is best to purchase a system with a CD-ROM drive.

- **Large appliances.** It's usually best to buy large appliances from appliance dealers rather than department stores, with large chains like Sears being the exception. Superstores, too, can also be competitive, but watch out: often times "supersales" at super-stores are little more than superhype. Shop around, and pay attention to the extras, like service, warranty, financing, and so on. Large appliances usually go on sale at the beginning of the year and early in the summer, so check the ads. *Consumer Reports Buying Guide* comes out in October every year—it is free for sub-scribers—and contains all the household items rated that year.

    With large appliances, you also have the option of buying used. You always take a risk when you buy anything used, but careful research can reduce that risk. Many stores specialize in used and rebuilt stoves, refrigerators, washers, dryers, and dish-washers. Prices usually begin at $100, including delivery and setup. Compared to the price tag for a new unit, that's quite a sav-ings. Plus, reputable shops will usually offer a limited warranty.

    If it's a real bargain you're looking for, nothing can beat the prices of used appliances sold at garage sales and in the classified section of the local newspaper. Keep in mind, you will have to transport the appliance(s) yourself when buying from a private party, and there is no guarantee. I'm sure many a junkyard has seen an appliance that broke down right after it was moved from one house to the next, but bargains can be bargains. I bought a used stove and refrigerator from a neighbor for $60 for the set, and they have lasted for years.

    If you opt for the big savings, it's best to buy an appliance that is currently being used rather than one that has been stored for a while. Although the seller may mean well, there's no telling what can happen while something sits idle, especially in a garage or musty basement.
- **Small appliances.** Like TVs and VCRs, small appliances may go on sale at any time. Keep an eye on sale advertisements and be patient. And as mentioned above, try to avoid appliances you won't use. I don't think there's a cupboard out there that doesn't have a juicer, deep fryer, bread maker, or pasta machine gathering dust.
- **Cars.** The first decision in buying a car is whether to buy new or

used. If you buy a new car, it's important to know that the car will depreciate as much as 25 percent the minute you drive it off the lot. This rate of depreciation varies, of course, depending on the type of vehicle you buy, the market value of that vehicle, and the price you paid for it. If you still want to buy a new car, here are a few quick rules.

(1) Negotiate up from the dealer cost, rather than down from the sticker price. New cars are generally priced 5 to 10 percent higher than the dealer invoice price. That may seem low, but dealers also make money from factory incentives, financing plans, and hold-backs, which are payments from manufacturers that can run as high as 5 percent of retail price. So in all likelihood, if you tell a dealer you want to pay 3 percent over invoice, you'll drive away in a new car.

(2) Watch the extras, especially extended warranties. A recent study on extended warranties on cars showed that 80 percent of the time, repairs needed during a warranty period cost less than the warranty itself. In other words, if you paid cash for each repair it would have cost less than the cost of the warranty. Also remember that many times the extended warranty is added to the sale price of the car, so you end up paying interest on that warranty for three to five years. You can, however, purchase long-term warranty insurance separately.

(3) Rustproofing and undercoating may not be necessary. New cars are treated at the factory, so, depending upon what part of the country you live in and how rough your winters are, you may not need additional protection. If you do, shop around for rustproofing at local body shops. It may cost far less than the dealer charges, and without the interest.

(4) Wait until fall—September to November—to buy a new car. At that time of year dealers are in a hurry to move out the old stock to make way for next year's models. Likewise, it's better to buy at the end of a month than in the beginning, and late in the day instead of the morning, for bookkeeping reasons. Remember, dealers want to sell you a car. Strike a bargain wherever you can, and don't be afraid to walk away. That's the good side of a free market economy, unless you like looking at blow-up gorillas and

listening to middle-aged men in bad suits holler about low prices while flailing their arms in every direction.

(5) Check *Consumer Reports* for information on the quality and performance of new car models, as well as dealer invoice prices, factory rebates, even tips on how to bargain with a dealer. Local credit unions, too, have valuable bargaining information on cars, such as blue book value, dealer cost, and factory rebates.

Of course, your best bet is to buy a used car, preferably two years old and still covered under warranty. Like used appliance dealers, used car dealers will often offer a warranty and provide proof of inspection, but you pay for that security. Buying a used car from a private party may be less expensive. With blue book values readily available, rarely will you happen upon a bargain that's too good to be true. Look for a good deal—a fair price for a car in good condition. Most private parties will not object to having a mechanic look a car over before you make your decision. Once you decide to purchase a car, all that's usually required is filing the change of title and a state inspection report with the county licensing office.

Often, people don't advertise a used car for sale; they just use word of mouth. So ask around to see if anyone you know knows someone who's selling a car. These are sometimes the best buys of all.

If you do decide to purchase a used car, there is an alarming nationwide trend you should be aware of. Some used car dealers, usually not very reputable ones, advertise used cars as though they were an individual selling a car. They place a classified ad with a phone number that leads to a pager or voice mail system, or they put a FOR SALE sign in the window and park the car in a parking lot or on an empty lot near a busy road or intersection. One person meets potential buyers when they call about the car, misrepresenting himself or herself as the owner of the car; and for all intents and purposes it looks like a normal, above-board transaction. But it is not. In fact, many such sellers have reset odometers, misrepresented cars' past accident records, and over-charged buyers.

- **Exercise equipment.** Thinking about buying a NordicTrack for the basement? How about a weight bench? In the world of exercise equipment there is one hard-and-fast rule: Don't buy new. A chain of health clubs could be furnished with equipment bought new and sold for a fraction of the cost by those who were determined that this time they'd get in shape. Watch the papers. When the thousands of dollars' worth of New Year's resolutions start collecting dust, usually around March or April, you can get equipment that's hardly been used, for just a few dollars. Likewise, people are usually looking for some extra cash just before Christmas. Most used exercise equipment is in excellent shape—especially if the piece was a good, sturdy one to begin with—and if you ever want to sell it yourself, you can get back what your spent, and sometimes even more.

Financing

ALL SORTS OF financing plans are available to buyers—low interest, deferred payments, deferred payments with low interest, deferred payments with no interest, and deferred payments with deferred interest, to name a few. These plans seem like good deals, and if used properly, they can be. For example, if you buy a refrigerator in August with $200 down and defer the remaining $600, interest-free, until the next January, you will be able to earn four months' worth of interest on that $600—that is, if you leave it in the bank.

Where couples get into trouble is not having that $600, or not being able to save it by payoff time (in this case, January), or spending it on something else. The interest on these "no-interest, no-payment" plans is actually higher than the interest charged by many credit cards. And the amount accumulates from the date of purchase, not from the date the final payment comes due.

A specific, albeit dated, example: In 1985, I bought a $1000 stereo, $200 down, at a big blowout stereo sale. By the time the payoff date rolled around, not only had I not saved the other $800, I had spent the $400 I had saved. I ended up financing the $800 with a large financing company, ITT Financial Services. It was my first exposure to such financing, and the payments over a five-year period were only going to be $33 a month, so I figured it was no big deal. But in five years, I would have paid $1980 for that $800. The total interest I would have paid, had I not figured it out eventually, was 147 percent of the amount financed—an interest rate of 44 percent!

The keyword here is, think. Think these plans through, payment by payment, month by month, year by year. Five years may not seem that long, especially with such low payments, but it all adds up. Add your total payments over the life of the loan. If companies are offering a low interest rate, compare that to the interest rate you could earn in a savings account or short-term investment; if the difference comes out in your favor, and if you trust yourself not to spend the money on something else in the meantime, you might consider financing.

Another option for financing purchases is credit cards. Some credit card companies offer money back, usually a percentage of your total purchases, at the end of the year. These cards are a good deal only if you get more money back than you've had to pay in interest or finance charges. GE Rewards MasterCard, for instance, now charges customers an annual fee of $25 if they don't pay at least $25 a year in interest charges. Other credit cards offer rewards, or discounts, off certain merchandise. For example, some cards offer points customers can accumulate to put toward purchasing "bargain" merchandise. These deals are like frequent flyer programs, in that the more you spend, the more points you earn, but unlike the free tickets you get from the airlines, customers can use points to pay for only part of the merchandise, so they often end up paying as much for the merchandise as they'd pay at a regular store.

Credit cards can be tricky for many people, particularly young adults or inexperienced consumers. Case in point: the latest trend in luring customers is the promise of low interest rates. But read the fine print. Often, that rate jumps up after an introductory period, usually three to six months.

The best way to use credit cards is to pay off the balance each month. That way, the cash you would have spent earns an extra thirty to sixty days' interest, plus, if your card offers money back, you get some cash back at the end of the year.

Telemarketing and Junk Mail

AS A NEWLYWED, you've probably been put on half a billion mailing lists. Many bridal shops sell their lists, as do bridal conventions, which collect names and addresses from free giveaway drawings. That means the phone calls and junk mail should start any day now (as if you weren't receiving enough already), trying to sell you everything from vacation packages to long-distance telephone services. And watch out, these professionals can be tricky. They may say something like, "To go ahead with this I just need to confirm a few things. Are you still living on Mead Road?" If you're not listening carefully, you may end up with aluminum siding for your apartment.

Solicitors for charities and civic organizations can also be mis-leading, saying, for example, they are collecting for a local fire depart-ment or children's softball team when they are really collecting for a city hundreds of miles away, or worse yet, a third party donating only a portion, if anything, of what they collect to that charity.

Your best bet is to mail your donation to the organization directly, or to check the solicitor identification carefully. And never, never, never give out personal information over the phone, especially your social security number. Companies will ask for it, but they don't need it and you shouldn't give it. Credit card information, address, marital status, income, buying preferences—this information is often requested during telephone surveys and to set up an account over the phone, so be careful. Before providing any personal information, be certain you know with whom you are dealing.

If you do make a substantial purchase over the phone, check to see if it is returnable, and how your money will be refunded (is there a non-refundable deposit or handling charge?). In many states, con-sumers are granted a cooling-off period after a substantial purchase—usually about three days—during which they can change their minds, return the merchandise, and get a full refund.

Resources

Automobiles

Organizations

Auto Safety Hotline
(800) 424-9393
Offers crash test results on specific vehicles.

Center for Auto Safety
2001 S St. NW
Washington, DC 20009
(202) 328-7700
Offers consumer protection information on new and used vehicles.

Publications

Consumer Reports Car Price Service
(800) 933-5555
Price reports on new cars are $12 for the first report, $10 for each additional report. Price reports on used cars are $10 each.

Edmund's 1997 New Car Prices and Reviews. El Segundo, California: Edmund Publication Corporation, 1997.

Edmund's 1997 New Truck Prices and Reviews. El Segundo, California: Edmund Publication Corporation, 1997.

Elliston, Bob. *What Car Dealers Won't Tell You.* New York: Dutton/Signet, 1996.

Gillis, Jack. *The Car Book 1997.* New York: HarperCollins, 1997.

Nerad, Jack R. *The Complete Idiot's Guide to Buying or Leasing a Car.* Indianapolis, Indiana: Alpha Books, 1996.

For more information on cars, www.edmund.com is an on-line service that provides dealer invoice price, as well as the value of many extras, on all new model cars and offers tips on negotiating.

General Purchases
Consumer Reports magazine
(800) 234-1645

Green, Mark. *The Consumer Bible.* New York: Workman Publishing, 1995.

Junk Mail
You can be taken off both mail and phone solicitation mailing lists simply by writing a letter to either of the sources listed below. State in the letter that you want your name taken off any mailing list presently being given out, and any in the future. Note: This will not stop those groups that solicit names from the phone book or guides that list phone numbers by address.

Mail Preference Service
Direct Marketing Association
P.O. Box 9008
Farmingdale, NY 11738-9008

Director of List Maintenance
ADVO
239 W. Service Rd.
Hartford, CT 06120-1280

❧ THE INVASION ❧

I was a stranger, and ye took me in.
—Matthew 25:35.

W hether you've been living together since junior high school or spent your first night together on your honeymoon, the agenda for the first year of marriage is pretty much the same. Just when you thought you knew your spouse better than your spouse knew himself or herself, you're really meeting each other for the first time.

There is something about the ceremony of marriage that changes the way people look at a relationship and themselves. In a study of couples who had lived together for seven to ten years before getting married, without exception, six months into their marriage, every couple reported feeling that their relationship was different now that they were married. The majority described this difference as a general sense of being happier and more secure than they had been before marriage. Strange, isn't it? Even after a ten-year period of mutual devotion and dedication toward one other, a simple piece of paper somehow changes everything. But because most couples don't expect life after marriage to differ from life before marriage, they are shocked when it does.

Many young couples tend to see married life as an extension of single life, with an additional person. You will continue to wake up on the couch to a blaring TV, put gum on the corner of the dinner plate to save it for later, and have friends over every weekend. And as long as you can tape your six soap operas during the day and watch them as soon as you get home from work, just as you always have, everything will be peachy. But as soon as two people step across the marriage threshold, with sweater-drying rack and dart board in hand, two sets of histories and expectations must join.

The English / First-Living-Together Dictionary

Words	Meaning
It's our place now.	You're not going to change anything, are you?
It just needs a woman's touch.	You get the gasoline and we'll torch the place for the insurance money.
Let's go out to eat.	I don't feel like cooking and I can't stand another of your bologna fondues.
No, I don't mind. Have fun.	You're leaving?!?
We need to figure out these bills.	I wonder if I can have QVC blocked from cable.
OK, we can make some changes.	Let's get another beer sign and a few more hockey posters.
You're not wearing that, are you?	You're not wearing that, are you?
Let me show you where the hamper is.	One more pair of socks left on the kitchen table and I'll kill you in your sleep and no court in the world will convict me.
Ready for bed?	Hubba-hubba! (sometimes)

The Invasion

PEOPLE WELCOME change "as long as things remain the same, or get better." But true change is welcomed about as much as having a tooth removed with a weed whacker. And even though you're going to be married to your mate for the rest of your life, does that mean you're going to have to live like he or she does? Does it mean you will have to start making your bed by throwing yesterday's clothes, which spent the night on the floor, on top of it? Does it mean having to wipe down the sink and tub after each shower so as not to leave any hair? Does it mean waking up every night as you're about to fall in the toilet because the seat was left up again? It's all part of learning to live together.

Studies of marriage show there is no correlation between an easy first year of marriage and living together prior to being married, but living together first does get a few of those put-the-old-milk-carton-in-front-of-the-new-one-so-we-use-the-old-one-first type of rules out of the way. Some of them, but not all.

The Invader

IF ONE PERSON is moving in with the other, the "mover-inner" is the invader. The invader understands the rules of the new world to be exactly as the native resident has stated: "Come here. Let's share this place. This is your place now. This is our new home." With this warm greeting the invader begins to establish himself or herself, creating a new home. However, the invader is trying to establish a colony where the native already has a culture, complete with language and traditions.

It is the purest form of human nature to envision oneself as the sole keeper of the truth, the one who knows how things should be done. One moves into a new home to straighten things out. "I'll show her the right way," the husband thinks as he surveys his wife's home, which is charming but in need of a man's touch. "It's a good thing I got here when I did. And don't bother to thank me now; I'm glad to help."

Or, the reverse scenario: the invader sees himself as a guest rather than an actual member of the tribe. Concerned with endangering the traditional ways or insulting the native, the invader may feel uncomfortable in his new surroundings. Sometimes, this discomfort is attached to the relationship itself, at which point the invader may begin to question its longevity.

The Invaded

THE INVADED, standing on the shores of her native land, greets the approaching newcomer with the purest of thoughts and the noblest of intentions, proud to share her rituals, routines, and land. Sometimes she waits with offerings: "Make yourself comfortable." "Shall we arrange the living room the way you had yours?" Sometimes with rules and regulations: "Stay on the rug protectors." "Don't disturb anything." "This is the way I've always done it." "Things are great the way they are, thank you very much." And the invader steps gingerly into his predetermined footprints in the carpet and walks along in the assigned manner.

Neutral Territory

NEUTRAL TERRITORY, seemingly, would be the answer for an easy transition. But in reality, both parties can play both parts, the invader and the invaded. Each wants everything to be new and exciting, but both need their own customs, traditions, and beliefs to be recognized and, preferably, followed. As a result, both partners can end up feeling like guests. The new territory is too neutral. It doesn't seem like home.

Of course, neither the invaded nor the invader is totally correct. It is impossible to establish a new home that is exactly like it was in two other homes. Likewise, it is impossible to create a home that fits both partners' expectations of what it should be. A marriage is a partnership. Both partners now form a team. A couple's new home will be a fusion of both spouses' traditions and expectations, or the adaptation of both partner's traditions and expectations with their new environment.

Identifying the Invader or Invaded Within

OFTEN, WHETHER the invader or the invaded, partners do not

articulate how and why, or even that, they feel frustrated. Because it somehow seems ridiculous, in the grand scheme of things, to be upset at having to sleep near the window, or to pout about work clothes getting wrinkled in such a small closet, each smiles and tries to let it go. Other times, they may not realize they feel that way. Following are some warning signs that you may be feeling like an invader, or the invaded.

Signs of Feeling Like an Invader
- Is reluctant to suggest compromises, or ways of doing things differently
- Keeps personal things packed away or leaves them in storage
- Avoids personal or family visitors, or phone calls
- Experiences periods of melancholy or sadness

Signs of Feeling Invaded
- Questions any change in ritual or routine
- Puts things back where they were before they were moved
- Thinks of several reasons *not* to change things
- Experiences periods of moodiness or irritability
- Suggests change only in specified areas ("Yeah, I don't mind if we change the extra bedroom.")
- Leans toward doing things simply because that's the way they were done before

The bottom line is, you and your spouse are fusing two lives together. You are mixing together forty or more years of combined experiences, traditions, and habits, so don't be shocked if there are some lumps in the batter.

Following is an exercise for communicating about and solving some of the frustrations that pop up in the first year of marriage. Even if a resolution is not reached right away, using this approach will help each spouse understand what is important to the other. It is a way of getting to know each other better.

1. Re-create your old life. Discuss with your partner your routines and ways of doing things, being honest about how well they worked.

2. Decide what about your old life was important, or what about

it made you feel comfortable.

3. Have your partner do the same.

4. If possible, fuse the two together. If the two do not mix well, compromise: you do this thing your spouse's way, and the next thing your way. Or, if this particular routine is important to both of you— be sure to save these for those things you cannot live without—try to work out an arrangement where you can each do it your way.

Clearly, this will not work for certain areas of your life together. For example, your finances would be a disaster if each partner was managing them differently. By and large, however, many things work out this way. One newlywed couple has separate bathrooms because they each have different routines in the morning and the neater spouse didn't want to have to nag the other about stepping on the rug with wet feet, cleaning up the sink, leaving the toilet seat in the proper position, and so on. They worked out a compromise for their daily routine, with the understanding that when they entertain guests each partner must clean his or her own bathroom.

What Type of Person Am I to Live With?
A Quiz

1. This is the third morning in a row that there's no hot water left for a shower. You:

    a. appreciate cold showers for the spiritual experience.

    b. take your shower the night before.

    c. ask your spouse to take his shower earlier.

    d. get up earlier and take a forty-minute shower and if there's still hot water left, leave the water running and do three loads of laundry.

2. A friend you haven't seen for a while calls and wants to come over. You:

    a. ask your spouse if she minds the company.

    b. say, "that's great because you haven't met my wife yet" and make it a group night.

    c. say OK, without asking.

    d. ask your spouse to go to the movies because you and your friend want to talk about the good old days.

3. After several attempts to get your spouse to pick up after himself,

there are socks, shoes, a newspaper, and a half-eaten sandwich left in the living room. You feel:

    a. neutral; it doesn't bother you.

    b. disrespected and discuss these feeling with your spouse.

    c. like the maid, angry.

    d. concerned about the authorities identifying the body.

4. You've had a hard day. You want to pick up a few videos, take the phone off the hook, and mentally turn off for a while. Your spouse had a great day and wants to go out or have friends over. You:

    a. get excited and go out expectantly.

    b. go out grudgingly and try to enjoy yourself.

    c. explain to your spouse your original plan and hope for a compromise.

    d. try to convince your spouse that what he really wants to do is stay home and watch *Terms of Endearment* with you.

5. Before you got married, you woke every morning to a blasting stereo to get you going. Your spouse is a light sleeper and doesn't have to get up until an hour after you. You:

    a. go cold turkey without the music and try to adapt.

    b. use a walkman.

    c. turn on the radio softly in the next room.

    d. move the speakers to both sides of the bed so your spouse will adjust faster.

6. You have a small lab of sprays, lotions, and tools for getting ready in the morning. There is only one little bathroom shelf, and it's full. You:

    a. operate out of a cardboard box for a while.

    b. weed out what you don't need.

    c. put as many things on the shelf as possible.

    d. break everything on the shelf and blame it on the cat.

7. You need some time alone. You:

    a. hope the feeling goes away.

    b. explain the need to your spouse in a loving manner.

    c. go off by yourself without asking.

    d. have someone call and say you were in a car accident, are being treated, and will be home at nine.

8. You can't sleep without the windows open. You:

a. try sleeping with them shut.

b. ask your spouse if she minds.

c. compromise, leaving them open part of the night.

d. nail them open so they can't be shut.

For every A answer you picked, you may consider yourself an understanding and easygoing individual. You don't count small rituals as all that important, and tend to put your partner's needs ahead of your own. Or, you're taking the test with your spouse in the room and will sneak back and take it later, answering more honestly. If the former, be careful not to discount your own needs so much that you feel resentment later on.

B answers show a thinking, diplomatic side. Your open, rational style will help you solve household situations with intellect and tact.

C answers show an ability for give-and-take. You hold your own traditions dear but are willing to compromise or change them when necessary.

D answers are the sign of a strong-willed individual who may someday need to join the Witness Relocation Program.

Don't Sweat the Little Things

BELOW ARE SOME of the most common issues in the first year of marriage, and some suggestions for how couples can deal with them.

- **Feeling at home.** Having a housewarming or a dinner party is a great way to make a new home your own, whether you have moved in with your spouse or the two of you have moved into a new home together. Having friends and family there to see you in your new surroundings can create a sense of pride in your home, and a feeling of ease and comfort. Sometimes it's the little things that help establish roots, such as being the voice on the answering machine, planting a garden, or making friends with the neighbors.

- **The slob factor.** If your spouse's housekeeping skills leave a bit to be desired, if clothes and dishes pave a path from the couch to the refrigerator, the pile method is a great alternative to bashing your spouse with a tire iron. The pile method simply involves picking a neutral location—a desk, a dresser, a closet, somewhere you can live with a mess—and placing all the wallets, car keys, dirty socks, magazines, dishes (if you have enough to spare), and so forth, in that place. This works for the "neatnik," because everything can be picked up and deposited quickly (you'll be picking it up anyway, just without the nagging), and it works for the slob because everything is in one place. Note, this is a *treatment*, not a cure.

- **The clash of expectations.** Sit down and discuss in detail how you expect your life as a couple to be. Maybe your mental picture is unrealistic. You won't know until it's out in the open. Be specific. Do you expect coffee to be brought to you in the morning like your father did for your mother? Do you expect your mate to be home exactly at 5:00? Do you expect to be able to have friends over every night? The majority of newlyweds' fights occur when one spouse is not acting the way the other spouse expects. But no one, not even Robert Duvall, can act without a script.

- **The age-old toothpaste dilemma.** This type of conflict is quite normal and really simple to resolve when you get right down to it. If your mate insists on leaving the cap off the toothpaste, or worse, squeezing the tube in the middle (gasp!), just buy two tubes of toothpaste. To solve the problem of whether to roll the toilet paper over or under (believe it or not, this actually accounted for an entire segment on *Oprah*), try installing two rollers. Of course, having separate bathrooms, as mentioned above, would not only solve both these problems but that perennial problem in the battle of the sexes: Should the toilet seat be left up or down? The best advice is just to get over it. Sure, you think the world would be a lot better place if your mate would just.... But would it really?

  Personal habits take some getting used to. Any two people need time to adjust to each other, a new lifestyle, and new surroundings. Relax. A routine will develop soon enough, and you will quickly forget that you were ever uncomfortable.

- **"Don't talk to me before I have my coffee."** There are morning people, and there are night people. And then there are peppy morning people. If you've married one of those people who pops out of bed, draws open the shades, and sings in the shower, first of all, my condolences. On the other hand, your mate is probably a happy person, which may be why you fell in love with him or her in the first place. Personalities come in many shapes and sizes; hence, the "through thick and through thin" clause.

- **"She never refills the ice trays."** Short of buying an ice maker or inspecting the ice trays daily, this type of personal annoyance can be overcome in much the same manner as the slob factor, explained above. Try leaving empty trays out on the counter. This will be particularly effective if your spouse happens to be persnickety about having an orderly kitchen. Of course, it still will not accomplish your ultimate goal: ice when you need it. Leaving friendly reminders, "Fill up the ice tray or die," may also get your message across, and may even go a long way toward fulfilling your ice cube fantasies; but more likely than not, you'll be fostering a resentment that will freeze your relationship sometime in the not-so-distant future.

  Empty ice cube trays are a common enough complaint that corporate America has come up with some innovative solutions, for a small price, including reusable ice cubes—plastic cubes filled with freezable liquid—and freezable glasses and mugs. Another simple solution is to buy bags of ice when you shop for groceries. Or, you can just make it yourself, and remind yourself how much your spouse does for you as you fill up the tray.

- **"Isn't the game over yet?"** Husbands watching sports all weekend is one of the most frequent complaints heard from newlywed women. While women often complain about their husband's sports-viewing habits, however, many women actually like watching sports on TV, particularly with their mates. Where couples run into trouble is when watching sports occupies the entire weekend.

  One possible solution is planning specific games and sports to watch, rather than just vegging out in front of the set watching anything that's on. Besides, if you're awake at 3:00 AM watching the European Boccie Ball trials, you may be a sports addict, in which case nagging may be the least of your problems. Here are some other solutions:

Have a sports party. Invite friends or other couples over to watch the game.

Participate in a sport together. Join a volleyball team or a bowling league. Take up tennis or golf. Being involved in a sport makes it more interesting to watch it on TV.

Go to the sporting event together. Rather than lounge in the easy chair all day Saturday, buy tickets to the local college football game and make a day of it.

Go do something else on your weekend time together, and listen to the game on the way.

- **Sharing the covers.** There's not much people can do to change their behaviors when they're fast asleep. Thus, newlyweds often complain about the spouse's snoring, hogging the covers, or kicking them in the middle of the night. There are some things both partners can do before falling asleep, however, that can reduce the occurrence of cover stealing. For instance, if the partner who steals the blankets dresses more warmly for bed—like wearing those sexy flannel pajamas—he or she may not be as likely to feel cold during the night. Likewise, if the partner who ends up without covers during the night dresses more warmly, he or she will not mind as much when the covers disappear. Another solution would be to keep an emergency blanket next to the bed so that whoever finds himself or herself without covers during the night can use a substitute blanket. For a more romantic option, try sleeping closer together. Body heat is better than a blanket any day.

- **"He never restocks the toilet paper."** This particular bad habit is common among both sexes, particularly those who grew up with brothers and sisters. There's a game most siblings play when it comes to using the last of something. Because the rule often goes something like "Whoever uses the last _____ (fill in the blank) must replace it," brothers and sisters develop a talent for leaving just enough of something to escape the technical definition of last user. For example, leaving three drops of orange juice in the container saved your husband, at one point in his life, from having to write "orange juice" on the shopping list. And that half a square of toilet paper on the roll probably meant that he didn't have to install a new roll, which as we all know can be an exhausting job.

Don't worry. There are some nifty gadgets on the market that can solve this problem. For example, using printed toilet paper, which comes in joke or trivia formats, could have you and your spouse racing to see who gets to change the roll. Not only that, having printed paper could replace those trips to the library, since you'll have all the reading material you need for the bathroom. There are also industrial-sized toilet paper dispensers on the market, which complicate the paper-changing process enough that it becomes a challenge he can't pass up. Some dispensers even come with a key.

- **"He leaves the toilet seat up."** Not to concentrate exclusively on matters of the bathroom, but it does seem a fair number of daily annoyances occur in that room of the house. (Maybe that's why most accidents occur in the bathroom.) As long as men have been raising the toilet seat to use the toilet, they have been leaving the toilet seat up, much to the chagrin of the women with whom they share a bathroom. Women complain that if they don't think to look before sitting down they fall into the toilet bowl, a particularly scary and annoying occurrence at two in the morning. Men ask why they should have to put the seat back down when they had to pick it up in the first place, thus doubling their work load. Both sexes have a legitimate point, unfortunately, so this struggle is not likely to resolve itself anytime soon. There is, however, an easy solution: keep the toilet seat and the lid down; that way, you will both have to lift and lower each time nature calls. What's more, you won't have to retrain yourself when Junior or Spot discovers the toilet in years ahead.
- **"She's a clicker fanatic. We can't watch even five minutes of a show before she's flipped to the next channel."** Watching more than one thing at the same time has become a popular pastime in this country. And for every person who clicks rapidly, it seems, there's a spouse beside him or her on the couch wishing the nonstop parade of flickering images and plot sound bites would stop. If you married the quickest clicker on the block, most likely you had an inkling before you said "I do." But dating

someone who can't watch an entire show straight through is a lot different from living with him or her, particularly if you only have one television set.

Which brings to mind the first possible solution: two television sets. That way, one can watch a show from beginning to end while the other flips channels to his or her heart's content. You could also purchase another remote control, one with a veto button. A surprisingly simple solution is, hide the remote. Chances are, your flip-happy spouse will neither sit next to the television set nor get up every five minutes to change the channel by hand. There are more sensible solutions, of course, but these involve communication. For example, plan your TV viewing ahead of time. Pick the shows you want to watch, and then watch them without interruption. Instead of flipping from channel to channel to see what's on, look through the *TV Guide*. Of course, the easiest solution—and the best one for your brain—is to turn off the TV and pick up a book. Perhaps a book about the first year of marriage.

WHEN THE PICTURES ARE BACK

Grow old along with me!
The best is yet to be,
The last of life for which the first was made.
                    —*Robert Browning,* Rabbi Ben Ezra

For more than a year, you have been moving at warp speed, organizing, planning, problem-solving, moving, and maneuvering. There have been things to do and places to be, with no time to spare. The wedding day approaches quickly. Next month ... next week ... tomorrow?

Tomorrow morning I'll cross-germinate those lilies and irises so I will have the perfect hybrid for the bouquet. Did I order a vegetarian plate for Aunt Emily? Did I call the caterers back to make sure that the Whitmans don't sit next to the Clawfields? Is there still construction on Baker Avenue? If there is, will the limos be able to circle around the church? If Carla doesn't come, I can invite David and Chloe. Has she R.S.V.P.'d? Where's the latest satellite photo of the Northeast? Looks like that storm front is moving out, so we may have a two-hour window to take pictures in the gazebo.

The time before a wedding is nuts. Plain and simple.

Couples should be able to put their wedding experience on their resume: *Negotiated critical issues diplomatically.... Streamlined and updated manufacturing procedure of wedding favors while increasing productivity and efficiency by 30 percent.... Acted as liaison between labor and management…. Successfully negotiated hostage crisis when reception ran out of coffee….* It's the equivalent of a part-time job.

The average time spent planning a wedding is between ten and fourteen months, which means that the two and a half million couples who will get married this year are, as we speak, doing their best to keep their jobs, friends, partners, and sanity as they tie up the last-minute details for their weddings.

Then suddenly the wedding is over, and it's back to hum-drumsville. Such an abrupt transition is a major life change in itself, without even considering all the other changes that go along with marriage.

Attention Withdrawal

UNLESS YOUR LIFE involves attending monthly Broadway openings or you're negotiating your newest video release, it's difficult to imagine a time when you've had more concentrated attention lavished upon you than before and during your wedding. For ordinary folk, it is probably the only time they get that much attention. It may represent their entire fifteen minutes of fame.

So after being in the spotlight, the star of the show, it's back to the chorus. The sales clerks are no longer rushing out to offer another veil, no more "account associates" are calling to see whether or not you've booked your limo yet, no more doting family members or friends are snapping pictures of your every expression. Celebritydom is over.

Planning Withdrawal

WHAT WAS THE EQUIVALENT of a part-time job is now a memory. You can now go directly home from work without having to stop at the tuxedo shop or the rental store to book the champagne fountain. But what should be a relief is actually a let-down for many people. It's difficult to adjust to traveling in first gear after racing around in overdrive for a year.

Some newlyweds try to adjust by taking on a lot of new activities. They start projects to reclaim that sense of accomplishment, but it's difficult to match the intensity and passion of planning a wedding. Any old project simply won't do. Enter, then, the quest for a home.

To many, looking for a place to put down roots seems the next logical step in Married Land—a pursuit that will offer the same rush that the wedding did. But watch out. Buying a house at the wrong time or for the wrong reason—namely, to feel excited about something again—can be a financial time bomb (buying a home is discussed in a later chapter).

If you feel the need to replace that wedding rush, don't look for another outlet, look for an *inlet*. Take some time for yourself. Relax for a while. Get back to those hobbies you put on hold for the wedding. Pay attention to areas in your life that you may have neglected in the last year: your family, friends, career, leisure activities.

Look at it this way: you pulled off a great success in life. You were able to put two hundred friends and relatives in one room, at one time, with minimal bickering and only one incident involving a firearm. That's a major accomplishment. The peace process in the Middle East should be so lucky.

And don't forget, you have a new spouse to concentrate on ("Oh yeah, I forgot about the love of my life").

Building a Life Together

THE FIRST YEAR OF MARRIAGE is a time for couples to relax and enjoy one other. Don't start on anything heavy just yet. Plan a weekend away. Take your time and find that perfect bed-and-breakfast in the country or that five-star hotel on the beach. Plan something reckless: go bungee jumping or white-water rafting or skydiving. Enter a bike race. Join a health club. Plant a garden. Write for tickets to be in the audience of a game show. Attend a major sporting event: the World Series, Kentucky Derby, or U.S. Open. Volunteer as a tutor, or walk dogs for the Humane Society. Throw a huge party. (On second thought, strike that one. Throwing a huge party is just the thing you want to do after spending ten grand on a reception, right? Best stick with the weekend away.)

Whatever you do, do it together. Find activities that you can both participate in. This is not to say you shouldn't have individual activities and goals. But it is important to share things with your partner at this time in your relationship. Now is the time to define and frame your life together.

This kind of sharing—the dreaded I-word, or "intimacy"—isn't always easy if you're used to personal ideas and goals being, well, personal. You have to remember that much of your life will now involve someone else, and if you don't share your goals or plans with your spouse, he or she may sabotage them without even intending to.

Let's say, for example, that without telling your spouse you've decide to lose ten pounds before your high school reunion in the fall. Great. You've been careful about eating right and exercising. You feel like you're heading in the right direction. Your spouse, who doesn't know about your goal, sees how hard you're working and decides to surprise you by preparing a romantic dinner for two, complete with French bread, wine, lasagna, cannoli—all that fattening stuff you've been avoiding. Because you don't want to hurt your mate's feelings, you eat the dinner (gobble is more like it), but end up feeling resentful at being pushed back three steps.

A formal conference or written plan is not necessary to let your partner in on a personal goal. A word in passing will usually suffice: "I think I'm going to stay away from red meat for a while." "I've got to start working on that project. Can you make sure I get up early for the next few weeks?" "I think I'm going to start running in the morning before work."

But then you must stick to it. You can't announce that you're going lose ten pounds, then come home the next night with pizza and a twelve pack, and get angry when your spouse wants to go out to dinner the next night.

"Didn't you listen? I told you I need to lose weight!"

"Oh, yeah. It must have slipped my mind between that third and fourth helping of potatoes at Thanksgiving dinner last night."

You've jeopardized your credibility.

The point is to communicate your personal goals with each other and then support one another in achieving them. That is your gift to each other.

Setting Goals Together

MOST COUPLES spend a year or longer, planning the big day, but not so much as a day planning the first year, or any other year, for that matter. Creating a life together is more than simply overlapping two established, separate lives, rolling along on a preset course. It is even more than blending those two lives, or building points of intersection into each course. Creating a life together is starting anew, setting goals and determining plans that both partners agree on and will strive for. It is taking up hobbies and pursuing interests that both partners enjoy. It is marrying someone as opposed to dating someone.

In addition to personal goals, try to set some mutual goals during your first year of marriage. Find some activities you can do together that you will both enjoy. Befriend other married couples and plan outings together. Use the following questions to get your brain storming.

1. **What have you always wanted to do? A hobby? An adventure?**
2. **Name something you've always wanted to do but have been afraid to try, or try alone.**
3. **Where have you always wanted to go?**
4. **What would you like to say you did when you get to work on Monday?**
5. **What is your favorite movie? Why? How can that be applied to your relationship? (It may reveal an interest, a passion, a goal.)**
6. **Where do you see yourself in five years? In twenty?**
7. **Where do you see you and your mate, as a couple, in five years? In twenty?**

Add your own questions to this list. The bottom line is, have fun. Talk to each other. Brainstorm with each other. Set goals together and see them through. Eventually you'll get used to being in civilian clothes again.

❧ CHORES ❧

This house … is clean!
—Spoken by Tangina, one of the parapsychologists in Poltergeist,
right after two people have been pulled from the netherworld
down through the living room ceiling

Chores. The mere mention of the word can cause children to run screaming down the block or hide in their closets. Husbands, too, disappear as if by magic when the word is spoken. Last-minute meetings come up (funny how they always seem to occur on the golf course), tools have to be replaced ("Honey, Sears is having a sale on just the screwdriver I've been looking for"), the cold/flu season begins abruptly ("I think I feel a sniffle coming on"). In my own marriage chores were a major issue the first year, one more indicator of how different my wife and I were.

My wife, Debbie, has the amazing ability to see dirt at the sub-atomic level. Hospitals and clinics regularly tour her apartment just to keep up on the latest sterilizing techniques. When we first met, this sort of obsession with cleanliness was alien to me. To put it mildly, I wasn't much into household chores. I mean, I knew that cleaning and chores existed. Now that I think about it, I may even have had friends who did chores. But other than that, I didn't have much to do with housecleaning.

Needless to say, right away in our relationship, a conflict developed. As I moved my private stock of lazy habits and rare jungle diseases into a stark, organized ecosystem that until then had known no predators, two worlds collided, and what a mess it was.

I'm happy to report that we survived. We are still married, and can say unequivocally that you will never see us on a domestic dispute episode of *Cops*.

In every relationship, to some degree, there's a neat person and a not-so-neat person. One may need to clean and organize; the other may not. One may want to do the dishes right after dinner, while the other has no problem waiting until tomorrow, or when the sink is full, or just skipping it entirely and deciding to move.

The dynamic that's created by the union of such disparate people, however, ends up encouraging the not-so-neat partner to be even less neat. Before he or she can get off the couch to take out the garbage or vacuum Sunday's crumbs, the other partner has already done it. "Cool, he's taking care of it. Now, where's that remote?"

For some couples, chores may not be an issue. There may be more pressing concerns than who cleans the bathroom or washes the kitchen floor. But for many couples, chores are a serious bone of contention. In fact, eight out of ten complaints in the first three months of marriage have to do with household responsibilities. Somewhere along the way, chores become a symbol of the status a spouse has in the relationship, a way of taking advantage of the other, or feeling taken advantage of. To my wife, for example, I was the most selfish, uncaring form of life on earth because I let my socks fall on the floor before I threw them in the hamper.

It is fairly easy to tell which role each partner will play, the picker-upper or the one being picked up after, by looking at each's history, position in the relationship, and personality.

History

WHERE YOU LIVED before you got married and your responsibilities in that environment are a sure sign of what your domestic inclinations will be in the future. For example, did you live with your fiancé? Did you live with your parents? Did you live alone? Or with roommates? If you survived living together before getting married, and you still wanted to get married, you probably have already worked through the sorts of problems that household responsibilities can create. More than likely, you're ready to fight about more important things now.

If you lived with your parents before you got married, the habits you developed there are the ones you'll take with you into married life. Look at your old routines: were you responsible for any part of the house other than your own room, and how strictly was that enforced? Did you do your own laundry, shopping, and grocery shopping?

If you lived alone, you were probably responsible for paying your own bills, cooking your own meals, cleaning your own house, and so on. But you also got to have everything the way you liked it. You had no rules other than the ones you wrote. Just because you lived by yourself doesn't necessarily mean you were the shining example of responsibility, though. You may have dropped your laundry off at your parents each weekend and picked it up on Sunday when you went over for dinner and to borrow money. Grocery shopping could have been replaced by the nearest free happy hour buffet or Pizza Hut delivery.

Most young couples today lived with roommates before getting married. Living in such an arrangement is paradoxical, because you're not living alone but you're not really living intimately with someone else, either. Having roommates does require a mix of both independence and patience, however, both of which are required in a good marriage.

Your personal history consists of the habits you have formed in your life thus far. But a habit can be formed or broken in as little as eleven days. So if you have a habit that you don't like, or that your spouse doesn't particularly care for—leaving toothpaste blobs in the sink or spattering hair spray all over the mirror, for example—there's still hope. Whether good or bad, habits, like rules, are made to be broken.

The Invasion Factor

HOW YOU FEEL about your new home and position in your home also influences the role you will play. Do you feel like a guest or a resident in your home? Are you the invader or the invaded? If you feel like the invader, you probably won't feel obliged to keep everything neat and organized. And if you feel like the invaded, you may have mixed feelings about sharing household duties with someone else.

Personality

NOT SURPRISINGLY, personality is the primary ingredient in the way people approach household responsibilities. While no two personalities are the same, some basic types are listed below. See if you recognize yourself.

- **Felix.** Organized, extremely neat. In high school, was elected captain of the vacuuming team. Alphabetizes grocery lists for more efficient shopping. Asks for Windex for Christmas. Knows date codes of spoilable food items and adjusts menus accordingly. Admires dental hygienists and carpet cleaners.
- **Couch Potato.** Ideal weekend involves less than forty minutes off the sofa. Enjoys motionlessness. Identification phrase: "Hey, they changed the schedule on the All Polka Network." Favorite sport: channel surfing. Dream purchase: satellite dish.
- **Party Animal.** Needs to run in a pack. Attracted to crowds. Still upset that friends couldn't come along on the honeymoon. Identification phrase: "It's not a party until something gets broken, you know." Favorite holidays: New Year's Eve, St. Patrick's Day, spring break.
- **Oscar Sloppy.** Needs time to clear out car seats when someone needs a ride. Is on the health department's Yellow List. Categorizes cleanliness of clothes in subtle degrees (keeping them separated in piles on the floor): clean, worn once, still wearable, getting there, almost done, one more time.
- **Mr. Benny.** Noted for thrifty nature. Believes lunch checks carry toxic diseases and won't touch them. Calls happy hours to see what all the free buffets are. Favorite activity: sneaking sodas and popcorn into half-price matinees.
- **Strategist.** Long-term planner. Talks of Christmas presents in July. Gets letter from IRS to wait until after New Year's Day to send in tax return. Requires a seventy-two-hour notice for any change in plans.

- **Gotrocks.** Convinced of independent wealth. Has memorized credit card numbers. First thing done on payday is picking up the tab for an office lunch. Has personal relationship with the UPS delivery person. Identification phrase: "I can't be broke. I still have checks."
- **The Cavalier.** Spontaneous. A fly-by-the-seat-of-your-pants type. Identification phrase: "How far of a drive is it to Mexico?" Noted for gleam in the eye when saying, "I've got an idea." Voted most likely to lose money in a pyramid scheme. Does Christmas shopping on December 24, when all that is open is 7-Eleven. "She likes coffee; I'll get her a travel mug, and a magazine...ooh, breath mints...."
- **Shecky Prankster.** Finds nothing funnier than physical, slapstick, practical humor. Favorite item: joy buzzer. Favorite holiday: April Fool's Day. Still tries to disguise voice when calling spouse.
- **Book Worm.** Has personal relationship with librarian. Has three books going at once. Perfect gift: bookshelves. Has reading material in car in case of traffic jams. Favorite TV episode: *The Twilight Zone* when Burgess Meredith gets trapped in a bank vault during a nuclear explosion and now can read forever with no one to bother him.

More than likely, you'll find elements of yourself and your spouse in several categories. Most people have found themselves in a last-minute shopping panic on Christmas Eve, even if the rest of their presents were purchased and wrapped by Memorial Day. So what happens when two different combinations mix? What happens, for example, when a Felix marries an Oscar?

I'm happy to say we've been married five years and are doing fine, thank you very much.

Opposites attract. Sometimes it may seem like you have a great deal in common; other times you may doubt that you're both native to this solar system. But why would you want someone exactly like you? You already have a you, what you need is a somebody else who doesn't have the same abilities and attributes that you do.

In this world or any other, there are no two people less alike than my wife, Debbie, and myself. I'm loud and obnoxious, she's polite and quiet. I'm spontaneous, she's a die-hard planner. (She was on the phone with her sister the other day trying to firm up lunch plans for three months from now, and frustrated because she couldn't get a commitment. Our Christmas shopping is done before Ground Hog's Day, and I think she has the college graduation outfit for our two-year-old on layaway.) She's organized, I'm a mountain of chaos. I like crowds, she likes cats. I'm a morning person, she likes Letterman. Of course, these differences are largely superficial. The really important things, like values and goals and beliefs and dreams, we share in common.

Different personalities manifest themselves in different ways, particularly when it comes to household chores. What usually happens, if the relationship is working, is one partner migrates to fill in the weaknesses of the other. If one is a slob, the other becomes less sloppy. If both partners have a tendency to procrastinate, one will begin to flex his or her organizational muscles by taking more of the responsibility. If both people are fairly irresponsible when it comes to paying bills, some bad credit and close calls will force the stronger of the two to pick up the financial ball.

Sometimes, these changes will simply happen. You'll wake up one day and be surprised to realize that you haven't been late on a single car payment in almost a year, when it used to be that making a car payment on time was cause for celebration. More likely, however, these changes will result from communication, negotiation, and compromise.

Compromise

EVERYONE HAS certain household jobs they don't mind doing and others they absolutely hate. One person may not mind doing laundry but hate doing dishes. The other may not mind doing dishes but hate cleaning the bathrooms. My wife, for example, doesn't mind washing the cars but hates rolling up the hose. Go figure.

Here's another one of those sit-down-at-the-kitchen-table opportunities for compromise. It may seem a little corny at first, but it works. Write down all the tasks that need to be done, separating them into categories: daily chores, like doing the dishes; as-needed chores, like taking out the garbage; weekly chores, like dusting and vacuuming the house and cleaning bathrooms; and seasonal chores, like cleaning the gutters and putting up Christmas lights. Include everything: the chores that are getting done now and those that are being put off.

Once you have each list completed, take turns picking chores that you don't mind doing. When you get down to the last few chores on each list, the worst of the worst, start negotiating. You can use the barter system, you can trade several lesser chores for one big one—anything you can both agree on that seems fair. Try your system for a while, maybe a week for the daily chores, a month for the weekly chores, a year for the seasonal chores. If something doesn't work, change it. No system has to be set for life. There is always room for future negotiation.

One newlywed pair started out their marriage blindly stepping into stereotypical roles—she cooked and managed the finances while he did all the yard work. After about six months of having to listen to him criticize her bookkeeping and her criticize the way the yard looked, they started talking about what each liked to do. It turned out he liked to cook and do the finances. She was relieved at not having to be responsible for balancing the checkbook and keeping track of financial details, which was never her strong suit as a single, and happily took over all gardening and lawn maintenance.

Another couple fought every weekend over doing the chores. Both worked full-time and didn't have the energy during the week to clean house, so they got up every Saturday morning, each dreading the next few hours, and trudged around the house picking up, vacuuming, dusting, and mopping. Finally they decided to hire a cleaning lady. They both made enough money to pay someone to clean the house, but because they had not sat down and talked about what they liked and didn't like, and how much they both hated housework—they had only negotiated what chores each would do—they had fought weekly for three years, assuming it had to be done and that they were the ones who had to do it.

A note of caution: By dividing chores you're sending a message that everything should be a fifty-fifty split, an attitude of "I'll do my half if you do yours." While this is an equitable way to go, certainly, there may be times when doing a favor or helping out your spouse is in order. Don't worry about crossing the yellow line. If the work gets done faster because you do more of it, there will be more time for the both of you. Besides, it all works out in the end. Don't get so caught up in an equitable division that you forget that your marriage is a union. In reality, the entire house is your responsibility, not just your half of it. You're a couple, a family, a team. It's community dirt now.

Remember, too, presentation has a lot to do with how your partner perceives your contribution. I remember when I was a kid and my parents would come home and ask my sister and me if we had finished our housework. I'd enthusiastically answer yes, reporting the tasks I had completed: "I:

1. cleaned my room,
2. did the dishes, and
3. raked the lawn."

My sister would jump up and say, "Yeah, but that's all he did. I:

1. went upstairs,
2. opened the closet door,
3. took out the vacuum cleaner,
4. brought it downstairs,
5. unhooked the cord,
6. plugged it in ..."

The Lazy Person's Guide to Choosing Household Chores

- **Mowing the lawn.** The greatest job for the terminally lazy: it looks hard and takes several hours, but involves little more than walking behind a machine in the sun (as long as you have a self-propelled mower). If you have a riding lawn mower, even better; mowing the lawn is like going on vacation.
- **Dusting.** Another easy job. Basically you just walk around the house and wipe off flat surfaces. Once in a while you have to lift some items, but they're usually small and light, so with a proper diet and exercise program you should have little difficulty.
- **Laundry.** Doing the laundry is a great job. It comprises three minutes of labor followed by an hour break: load the washing machine and wait until it's done; unload the washing machine, put the load in the dryer, and take another break; unload the dryer, fold the laundry, put it away, and take another break. An

hour and a half job that requires six minutes of actual work!

- **Dishes.** Doing dishes has gotten a bum rap over the years, but it's really not a bad job. It does involve real work and constant motion, but you get to keep your hands in soapy water and play with that squirty thing on the back of the sink. Think of it as a partial bath.
- **Cooking.** Women have guarded this secret closely over the years, sharing it only with some male chefs along the way—although with those funny hats, it's no wonder more men haven't picked up on it. Cooking is actually quite enjoyable, and offers the fringe benefit of instant gratification (assuming the meal turns out like it's supposed to). The downside is that most part-time cooks do not know how to exercise the culinary arts in a clean and organized manner. The kitchen ends up looking like the food fight scene in *Animal House,* so that clean-up requires dragging in the fire hose, hosing everything down, and rolling that cumbersome hose back up.
- **Vacuuming.** Pushing a machine, which is often self-propelled, over a soft carpeted area—that's a tough one. The only negative part is having to move furniture and large debris out of the way before you begin. But that can be negotiated as a separate chore if you're clever enough. Vacuuming also involves a sort of instant gratification: "Oh, you vacuumed in here, didn't you." "Yup, I vacuumed the entire house." "Wow, thank you."
- **Picking up.** Pre-vacuuming, or picking up, can also be a great job because it's an opportunity to be creative in your housework. You can put things in areas you hadn't thought of before. "Where can I put these newspapers? Under the couch! Yeah. And these books can … go in the freezer!" You may even find that wrench you've been looking for since last October.
- **Cleaning the bathroom.** Though it's one of the least pleasant chores, cleaning the bathroom is the ultimate job for those inclined to laziness. The bathroom is usually the smallest room in the house, yet it qualifies as an entire room. It has the least amount of floor and countertop area, and rinsing can be most enjoyable. Plus, wearing rubber gloves goes a long way toward protecting you from cooties.

- **Grocery shopping.** Another of those somewhat fun jobs, grocery shopping enables you to get out of the house, possibly bump into someone you know, and even browse for a while in the magazine aisle if the pressure builds up. Plus, you get to push a little cart around and practice your traffic-weaving skills. If you're really out for a good time, try calling on one of those little red phones at the end of the aisle to ask where certain items are. If the grocery store is full-service, you may even be able to get away with asking the person on the other end of the phone to bring the items to you at the juice counter or in the coffee shop.
- **Ironing.** Ironing is like mowing the lawn. You move a smooth metal plate over soft, smooth clothing. Because it takes so long, however, you can claim you're totally exhausted when you're through, down some Gatorade, and take a nap.

    So, while you're negotiating your chore compromise, remember this: just because something looks difficult doesn't mean it is. Try out different chores, and see which ones you think you can master without breaking a sweat. Best be on guard for your spouse to do the same, however.

Chore Negotiation: An Exercise

1. Fill in the categories below with chores that need doing around your home. Include everything, even if you are already agreed on who does it. You need a complete list to begin your negotiation.

Daily Chores

_____
_____
_____
_____
_____

Weekly Chores

_____
_____
_____

_____

_____

Periodic Chores

_____

_____

_____

_____

_____

Seasonal Chores
Winter

_____

_____

_____

_____

Spring

_____

_____

_____

_____

Summer

_____

_____

_____

_____

Fall

_____

_____

_____

_____

2. Using each chore you listed in Step 1, divide the chores between yourself and your spouse. Take turns selecting a chore, leaving those you like least for the last. Write them under your name in the table below.

HIS	HERS

3. Once you are down to the least desirable chores, negotiate. For example, "If you will clean out the gutters each spring and fall, I'll mow the lawn for the entire summer." When you've divvied up each chore on the list you completed in Step 1, fill in the columns below.

HIS	HERS

MEN DON'T WEAR UNDERPANTS

O Lord—if there is a Lord; save my soul—if I have a soul. Amen.
—*Ernest Renan,* Prayer of a Skeptic

To this day, the word *underpants* drives me crazy, and don't think my wife doesn't know it. She knows, believe me. If I've told her once, I've told her a thousand times, they're called underwear, underwear, UNDERWEAR!

Ours is just one of those silly language differences you notice once you're married. And with different expressions, some more annoying than others, come different traditions as well. "You mean to tell me that your family didn't watch *It's a Wonderful Life* on Christmas Eve, open one present, then drink hot cider and sing 'Oh Danny Boy?' You're kidding me! It wouldn't be Christmas without that."

Every family has its own history and experiences, its own traditions, values, and language. The family rituals you grow up with seem natural to you—the norm. Doing anything else seems alien, uncomfortable. Christmas isn't real without.... It doesn't seem like the Fourth of July without.... What's Thanksgiving without...? We always dressed up for....

When you marry someone from a different family, two sets of traditions, values, and expressions collide. The more disparate the traditions or values, the bigger the collision. For example, my wife's family dresses up when they fly anywhere. Riding on an airplane is a formal occasion that requires formal attire. When my wife and I were packing for our first real vacation, Debbie laid out dress clothes, while I selected a pair of khaki shorts, beat-up sneakers, and my faded 1983 U.S. Open T-shirt. We had reached a conflict of customs.

And because my parents were brought up during the Depression, I was raised to believe that you don't buy anything that doesn't perform at least sixteen or seventeen functions. "You don't have to buy curtain rods; I've got some broom handles and duct tape in the basement. Give me ten minutes." Once again, my idea of normal was in direct contrast to my wife's, whose family routinely purchased a separate trinket for every possible operation to be performed. "Don't buy those curtain rods, they're for French-style windows."

A couple from my workshop were encountering problems celebrating Thanksgiving. In one spouse's family, the men drank beer and watched football on TV the entire day, while the women prepared and served the meal, cleared the table, cleaned up the kitchen, and then chatted among themselves into the evening. The other spouse's family had a different tradition. Everyone—women and men alike—helped clear the table and do the dishes, and the entire family sat together after the meal and played board games.

At times, a new spouse may seem to be from another country. Take language, for example. Even if both partners are English-speaking, or at least profess to be, words and phrases used by one spouse may be unfamiliar to the other spouse. You know that little area on the passenger side of the car, the place you put things? Is that a glove compartment or a glove box? Do you cut the grass or mow the lawn? Is that long sandwich in your hand a hero or a sub? Do you drink soda or a pop? Do you take your coffee light and sweet, or with cream and sugar? And if your husband says he'll be home after dinner, will he be home at two, or seven? Some families call the evening meal, dinner, and other families call it supper. These latter families do eat dinner, however; it's what they call the noon meal on Sundays and holidays.

Clearly, such differences are trivial, especially when both partners love and respect one another. But words may cause problems in a marriage because of the images they conjure up. Some people have preconceived notions about people from certain regions of the country. Accents and expressions common to these areas will elicit assumptions and attitudes about the people saying them. For example, certain northerners are raised to believe that most southerners are slow—after all, it's so hot down there, they avoid working up a sweat, don't you know—and that southern women, those Southern belles we've all heard about, are raised to compete for men and will stab you in the back sooner than lose out on a "good catch." Clearly, these stereotypes are no more accurate than stereotypes about New Englanders being cold and tight-fisted. Yet one quick "y'all" can forever shape an impression, and sometimes a relationship.

Family Traditions

FAMILY TRADITIONS are often the most important traditions, because they involve the magic and fantasy of childhood. Childhood memories are far more exciting and powerful in the mind's eye than any event could possibly be in adulthood. In addition, many family traditions are tied in with holidays or special events and reinforced by religious and ethnic traditions.

Probably no two families celebrate Christmas exactly the same way. Some open their presents on Christmas Eve, some on Christmas morning, and some on Christmas night. Some have lobster stew, some have turkey, some have toad-in-the-hole for Christmas dinner. But when two people marry, two diverse traditions must somehow fuse into one, a process that is often uncomfortable. It may not feel right, for example, to be at your new in-laws' house opening presents in your pajamas and robe at 8:00 AM when you are used to waiting until after Christmas dinner.

People remember childhood traditions with a certain poetry, a certain magic, that is missing from traditions created later in life. Thus, many newlyweds cling to their early memories and family traditions fiercely. But in marriage, compromise is often the name of the game, as you probably already know. Sometimes you may have to choose one tradition over another, just as you may have to choose which family to spend certain holidays with. But be careful. Choosing families and family traditions can be dangerously close to saying one spouse's family is more important than the other's.

Special Events

SPECIAL EVENTS are different from holidays. Special events are the graduations, recitals, pool parties, and family reunions that start filling weekends beginning in May, and don't seem to stop until mid-October. Because they do not fall on specific times of the year like holidays do, you can expect your family's special events to conflict with your spouse's family events from time to time. More than likely, you will have to be out of town or have promised a friend to help him move the very weekend of your spouse's bi-annual family reunion or second cousin's graduation.

Depending on your families, and the importance of the event, such conflicts may or may not be an issue. More than anything else, it seems to come down to time management, which is so important it gets its own chapter later on. But I want to touch on a few things quickly. For starters, how did you and your spouse, then your fiancé, schedule these types of events before you got married? Did you visit one set of parents one Sunday and the other set the next? How about on Father's Day? Or Mother's Day?

Though each side of the family is equally important, it is dangerous to split family time fifty-fifty. Often, a decision will have to be made. And rather than get into a "last time we did your family's thing, so this time it's my family's turn" type of arrangement, it's best to prioritize the events, and let each event's priority determine where you will go.

For example, one couple set up a system that ranked events in order of importance: a health-related event, such as a birth, took precedence over all else, followed by religious events like weddings and christenings, then birthdays, then recitals and seasonal programs such as Christmas concerts and graduations, particularly for young nephews and nieces, and then other family get-togethers like a Fourth of July picnic or family reunion. If two equally important events fell on the same date, the couple came up with another ranking system to decide which to attend that included the age of the person the event was for, whether or not promises had been made, the importance of the event to the individual(s) involved, the closeness of the relationship with the individual, and how many times they had missed an event for that individual before. When they scheduled events, they also talked openly about which they wanted to go to, and if all else failed, they each went to their family's event and made excuses for the other.

Religious Traditions

FOR SOME families today, an interfaith marriage is still a contentious issue. I remember my mother telling me that when she and my father were dating in the '50s and he brought her to meet his parents, my grandfather's only requirements were that she be neither Catholic nor Democrat. Well, he had to settle for one out of two (she's a committed Democrat).

Some of the difficult decisions couples of mixed faiths face include planning the wedding ceremony (Will it be Jewish or Catholic, or Catholic with full Mass?), choosing their children's faith, and deciding which holidays to observe. Deciding which holidays to observe, of course, goes a long way toward determining *how* those holidays will be observed and with whom.

Religious traditions should be discussed openly and frankly both before the wedding and throughout the marriage. Often, people feel estranged from their religion when they are young. Later on, however, especially after children have entered the picture, they may want to reconnect with their religious roots.

Ethnic Traditions

THERE ARE 106 different ethnic groups in the U.S. There are also more than 1 million interracial couples in the United States. Though this country has come a long way in the last thirty years in terms of racial understanding and tolerance—far enough, at least, to be home to so many interracial couples—we clearly haven't come far enough. Interracial couples still report that the major difficulties in their relationships are external.

For example, many interracial couples report that reactions from family, friends, and even co-workers create tension in their relationship. They must fight for their relationship as soon as it becomes "serious." Even those families that don't exhibit obvious prejudice are sometimes taken aback at the idea of their child marrying someone from a different race and culture. Some families still draw a line between sitting next to someone from a different ethnicity on the bus and being related to that person. Their objections to interracial marriage may be disguised as concern for the couple's feelings: "You know people will stare and wonder, don't you?" "How will your son or daughter feel when he sees that all the other kids' parents are the same color?" "What will people say?"

There's no getting around the tensions and outward difficulties of being in an interracial relationship. Just to know ahead of time that it may be an issue, and to know how you'll react, is half the battle. And, of course, maintaining open and honest communication, and supporting and loving one another.

Personal Traditions

PERSONAL TRADITIONS are often negotiable in ways that family traditions are not. Before I got married, one of my favorite personal traditions in the fall was making my famous junkyard chili. On the first truly cold weekend of autumn I'd go to the store to get the ingredients: fresh peppers, onions, tomatoes, and meat. Then I'd go home, make the appropriate phone calls, and begin cooking. The chili took all day to make. Starting in the morning, the ingredients would simmer slowly as friends trickled in with their offerings of fresh bread, taco chips, and beer. By the time the football game had started, the air was thick with the smell of cooking peppers and Tabasco. Throughout the afternoon we'd sample the sauce until it was finally ready in the early evening. Then we'd all eat several bowls of chili while we watched football and talked.

When Debbie and I got married, we continued this tradition. The first year we invited a few friends over and had a lot of fun. The next year we invited fewer people, and the next, even fewer, until finally it was just us. The tradition is still a symbol of autumn and it's still just as fun. But now I focus more on keeping Nick, our two-year old, from pulling the chili pot over his head than on getting the sauce just right. Because junkyard chili that once took all day to make really can be done in about twenty minutes.

From the outside, changing a tradition like this may seem like a loss, but it's not. It's the evolution and growth of a new family. That one tradition changed and hundreds of new ones grew.

New Traditions

ALL TRADITIONS evolve naturally. Your childhood was different from that of your parents. Your parents' childhoods differed from their parents'. Things change, governments collapse, technologies expand. The traditions you grew up with were, to some extent, new traditions that had evolved in your parents' house out of the traditions they had grown up with, and now new traditions will evolve in your house. And then those traditions will evolve when your kids leave home and make their own traditions with their new families.

Often, a tradition doesn't do well when it's transplanted from your parents' home to your married home. The transplanted tradition lacks vitality or strength. Christmas Eve may not feel right, for example, without the sounds of kids. Neither partner enjoys the activity or occasion as much as they used to, and over time the tradition dies. Instead of trying to transplant all their traditions, newlyweds need to encourage new ones to grow. This is not an onerous task. Creating your own family traditions pretty much just happens. I don't know of many couples who sat down and tried to create a tradition involving the first snowfall or Saint Patrick's Day. Sometimes how these traditions came to be is what makes them stick. One year you waited until the last minute to get the fixin's for Christmas dinner. The car broke down, so you had to walk three miles to call a cab. By then all the stores were closed, and the only thing open was a deli, and that's why you always have pastrami at Christmas.

If certain traditions are important to you, discuss them with your spouse. There's always room for negotiation as long as you are both willing to compromise. Like the process outlined in an earlier chapter for divvying up chores, start with the traditions most important to you and work from there. You probably don't need me to tell you that, but it may ease the struggle in the beginning. It's natural to struggle with traditions. Relax. Have fun. And if you're looking for something to do, I'll send you my chili recipe.

DEALING WITH THE REST OF THE WORLD

I propose to fight it out on this line if it takes all summer.
—Ulysses S. Grant, to General Henry Halleck, May 11, 1864

Outsiders have a way of creeping into a new marriage fairly early. After all, everyone has relatives, friends, co-workers, old neighbors, acquaintances, and schoolmates in their lives. And these outsiders all require time and attention. They have stress in their lives they need to talk about, their kids have holiday programs to go to, their annual Super Bowl party is a must-attend. Just getting to know all the other people in your mate's life can be difficult enough. When it comes to balancing time spent with outsiders and time spent together as a couple, though, just "difficult" would be nice.

Family

THE FAMILY BOND is the first relationship human beings have. Family is a person's lifeblood, literally—an extension of one's self. No other people on the planet know how to pull your strings like the members of your family.

Because most people are raised counting on and being close to their family—even in the case of stepparents, most children are closer to one family and one parent than the other—it can seem very strange, in the first year of marriage, to be asked to adopt a new family. Suddenly you are asked to take on a second, perhaps conflicting set of familial priorities. You now have "my family," "your family," "my family that's now your family," "your family that is now my family," and "our family—that is, you and me." That's a lot of families, not to mention relationships, to keep up with.

In the first year of marriage no topic provokes more fights than family. Well, maybe money. And chores, too. But family is definitely in the top three. If for some strange reason you're having trouble getting a good fight started about either of your families, try one of the following phrases. They're guaranteed to get the juices flowing.

"I saw your sister on the highway today, and I swear there were flying monkeys guarding her car!"

"I'm just going to leave my wallet outside the door, so there's no need for your brother to actually come inside the house."

"I'm mailing Christmas cards today. Shall I send your father's to the warden's attention or right to his cell?"

"I was flipping through Revelations the other night and read all about your mother."

"To save time, I've had a third of my paycheck deposited directly to your sister's bank account."

"If your niece comes over, do you think she can find some truffles for us?"

As much as television sitcoms and comedians poke fun at in-laws, however, most people get along with their spouse's families. According to *Statistical Handbook on the American Family* by Bruce A. Chadwick and Tim B. Heaton, 75 percent of all couples in a national survey said their relationship with their mother-in-law was good. About 68 percent reported that their relationship with their father-in-law was good.

The Ogre in the Family Album

Of course, there is always a possibility that you and someone in your new family may not exactly enjoy each other's company. As the saying goes, you can pick your friends but you can't pick your family. So what do you do if you would like to wish on your brother-in-law the slow, agonizing torture of being covered in butterscotch and left near an ant hill?

Occasionally, the reason for disliking an in-law is justified. You find out, for example, that the weekend before your wedding your sister-in-law brought your wife's ex-boyfriend along on an outing, "just to see if there was any spark left." You may even be picking up on your spouse's hatred of his or her own relative, the possible reasons for which are far too numerous and complicated to explore in this book. More often than not, however, disliking someone is simply an uncomfortable feeling you get around that person ("I don't know what it is, but I just don't like that guy"), or even a reaction, or over-reaction, to an incorrect assumption. ("I know your dad hates me because he can't even look at me when I'm talking to him." Never mind that he has trouble focusing on anything for any period of time since his accident.)

Although people tend to think of themselves as complex, controlled individuals, most people are fairly transparent. It's difficult to dislike someone and not have them pick up on it. For that reason, it is wise to try to find something you like about your in-laws, some common ground or interest you can discuss whenever you see them.

As an experiment, try this: If someone in your spouse's family is difficult to get along with, pretend you like that person the next four or five times you see him or her. Two things will begin to happen: First, you will enjoy your time with that person more. When you act like you're enjoying something, it's nearly impossible for that feeling not to kick in sooner or later. Before you know it, you won't be pretending. The second thing that will happen is, you will notice the tension dissipate between you and this person. When you have fun with someone it is hard not to like them. If nothing else, you can concentrate on the fun you've had together.

Try this with your sister-in-law, your father-in-law, even your spouse's loud-mouthed cousin, and see what happens. If after half a dozen tries you still don't like the person, just be as civil as you can. There's no rule that to have a happy marriage you must adore every one of your in-laws, although it would probably help. Families come with more than enough tension. It's wise not to create more if you can help it.

The Super-Divorced Family

Not too long ago—as recently as 1980, in fact—the divorce rate in this country was much higher. Today, it is on the decline: nearly one-third fewer divorces were filed last year than fifteen years ago. This trend can be explained in part by yet another trend among young adults—where would we be without statisticians and trend spotters?—namely, that they are waiting longer to get married. The average age of a bride last year was twenty-six, and the average age of a groom was twenty-eight. Compare that with 1982, when the average age for a bride was twenty-two, and for a groom, twenty-five; or 1972, when it was twenty for a bride, and twenty-three for a groom. In 1960 (back when dinosaurs roamed the earth and your parents were probably getting married), the average age of a bride was nineteen and a groom, twenty-one.

While encouraging, the declining rate of divorce does not mean that you won't be affected by divorce in some way. Even though your marriage stands a better chance of surviving than your parents' did, there's still a very good chance that members of your family will divorce and remarry once, or even twice. That's four stops instead of two on holidays. And that's two times the potential for problems brought about by interfering in-laws and twice the likelihood that there will be someone with whom you'd rather not spend time.

And as if that weren't enough, there is always the lingering tension created during a divorce that bites back at every opportunity. "Oh, I see you're going over to your *mother's* house for Thanksgiving. Any chance we could steal an hour or two of your time?" Of course, if you got through the wedding with your heads intact, you've already proven that you have negotiating skills that any United Nations representative would envy.

Friends

WHAT ARE FRIENDS, besides those individuals with whom you'd jump off a bridge if they did (and your mother thought she was asking a rhetorical question)? They're an extension of who you are. Your friends are connected to you. They allow you to see yourself, and other aspects of life, through their eyes.

Each marriage is unique when it comes to friends, as unique as the marriage itself. For many people, friends were substitute spouses before they got married, playing the parts of confidence builder, career adviser, court jester, banker, confidante. Some people run in packs. Others have a few close friends. Still others find all the companionship they need in their spouse. Problems arise when one spouse has a different view of friendship than the other. Remember, opposites attract—and then they get married.

When you married, in addition to inheriting a new family, you also inherited a network of friends. Childhood pals, acquaintances, blood brothers, fishing buddies, "how are ya?" friends from the health club, old romantic interests who are now "just friends"—everyone in both of your lives is now part of your life together. You now have "my friends," "your friends," "my friends that became your friends when we got married," "your friends that became my friends when we got married," and "our friends."

There are three basic types of friends: close friends, work friends, and acquaintances.

- **Close friends** are those with whom you have strong emotional bonds. Usually, although not necessarily, this bond has developed over time. Sometimes you just click with someone, and six months later they're in your wedding. For many, the way they feel about their close friends is similar to the way they feel about their spouse.

- **Work friends** are those people you spend eight or more hours a day with. These are the people who work in the trenches with you, solving problems, achieving goals, being tormented by the same supervisor. On an average work day people spend only four hours with their spouses, half the time they spend with the people at work. Work friends, naturally, become a big part of your life, even when you don't socialize outside of work. Like it or not, that work friend you occasionally talk about over dinner is now part of your marriage.

- **Acquaintances** are individuals who know you by face, but struggle to recall your first name because they never knew your last. Acquaintances serve as another source of information and opinions on the world—or simply the side of town you don't normally frequent. "Remember that guy ... Chip, from the golf course? He says Marloni's has the best minestrone in the city. Let's go there."

All together, it's a lot of people to deal with. Especially since all demand some time and effort. Couple friends, for example, are friends who have mates who get along with your mate, and you do things together as couples. This uncontrollable urge to associate with couples is especially strong in the first year of marriage, and still a topic of debate among scientists. It has something to do with being able to respond to the universal question asked Monday morning at offices around the nation—"What'd you do this weekend?"—with something interesting, like, "Oh, we went skiing with Chris and Diane, some friends of ours."

Socializing with other couples can be beneficial to your relationship. Among other things, spending time with another married couple can provide an alternate view on marriage, or even point to an alternative way of life. However, some couples go so far as to design complicated campaigns to recruit other couples to do things with, all too often ignoring whether or not they share common interests or hobbies with the other couple. Acquiring couple friends can even become a relay of status or stature, where the wealth or social standing of couples determines their status as friends. Some couples seem to define themselves by the type of friends they have: that Charles is an airline pilot and his wife, Tricia, is a fashion designer somehow is supposed to make their own lives interesting or important.

Another category of friends are old chums, dear friends you've had most of your life, who will get to know your spouse but will remain your friends. These are the friends you can call when you've had a fight with your mate and they'll automatically take your side. These are the friends with whom you plan weekend getaways, "no spouses allowed." These are the friends you will most likely have for the rest of your lives.

Of course, if you can make the transition from "your friend" or "my friend" to "our friend," that's ideal. My best friend from college is now "our friend" and my wife's closest friend (she doesn't get out much). But that's pretty rare. Most likely, you will each have close friends with whom you spend time alone. That's fine, as long as you are able to balance the needs of these relationships with those of your marriage.

Setting Ground Rules

TO BALANCE your own needs with those of your family and friends, whatever their type or category, it is sometimes necessary to draw a line in the sand and not cross it under any circumstances. This is often the case with overbearing in-laws, who want to be updated daily about the goings-on in your relationship, family planning, career progress, whatever they can pry from you that falls under the classification of "none of your business." Or close friends who still expect the amount of time from you that you spent together in high school, before a full-time career, before marriage, before you had four kids and joined the neighborhood car pool. There are separate rules for family and friends, as it should be. Each are explained below.

Family

Unless you come from a clan like that featured in *Goodfellas,* it probably won't be necessary to skip town to avoid unwarranted intrusions from your family. It may, however, be in line to bring the heads of all the families together to serve notice: "From now on, don't drop by unannounced after eleven, please."

Setting up rules can be tough. Relatives can take offense easily, particularly if they don't understand your need for privacy or acknowledge the authority of your own house rules. But remember, you and your spouse are your own family now, and you deserve to be respected as such. You're no longer dating or seeing each other or engaged; you are a married couple with your own home, apartment, trailer, tee pee, or igloo. And the rules that govern that space are yours to set. If you don't want family members storing things in your garage, borrowing whatever they feel they need, rummaging around in your refrigerator for leftovers—whatever charming habits your family members have—you have the right to say so. But you do have to say so. Your father-in-law isn't going to know that you don't want coffee and rolls brought over Sunday morning at 7:30 if you don't tell him.

Once you've decided how you want things to be, inform your

family. If you're looking for a tactful way to tell them, especially if your line in the sand will be a departure from the way things are now, there's always the "I have a friend who always calls early on Sunday morning" approach. Explain your "friend's" behavior and recount the way you stated your rule to him or her. You might even ask your in-laws' advice at that point: "Do you think I hurt his feelings? Do you think she understood?" With a little luck, your in-laws will be bright enough to figure out the parallel without you having to supply the link. If you do have to spell it out, however, honest communication is always best. Talk openly and specifically about those things that are causing you tension. Chances are, the perpetrators don't realize what they are doing, or that what they are doing annoys you.

Once you've aired your concerns, try to negotiate new behavior by using the following four steps:

1. Draw the line. Establish your bottom line, what you absolutely will not tolerate—showing up, unannounced, at 7:30 in the morning and walking in your bedroom without knocking, for example. Just as they have absolutes you must abide by, the same goes for them. And you have a right to hold them to their word.

2. Be fair. It's important to set rules, but they have to be fair to all sides. Do not tolerate from your side of the family something you would not tolerate from your spouse's. Ground rules must be your absolutes, not different hoops to jump through depending on who is doing the jumping. Nor should ground rules be changed for the side of the family that screams the loudest.

3. Don't talk to one family about the other. Even if your families have had the most civil and understanding divorce in the history of mankind, complaining to one side about the other can still cause trouble. Though it may be difficult to do at times, remain neutral.

4. Always be respectful. Even if their behavior is thoughtless and inconsiderate, they are still people and deserve your respect. They're your people, for that matter, whether you want them to be or not. Save yourself hurt feelings and resentments later on by simply respecting that they have the right to behave the way they want to— just as you have the right to tell them to stop.

5. Try to spare feelings. Tell your family members you care about them before you start talking, and after. Start on a good note and end on one

Friends

Most newlyweds seem comfortable with the notion that they will see things differently in the beginning of the marriage. They accept that they will need time to synthesize their viewpoints about the role money and chores, for example, will play in their new life together. Then why do so many newlyweds expect their spouses to immediately share their attitudes about their friends?

It may be that when you meet someone and fall in love, you fall in love partly with the way that person treats other people. You get to know your mate's friends along the way and see how they interact with each other. But once you're married, like it or not, relationships change. You become the first priority in your mate's life, not his or her friends. Friends fall anywhere from number two to number ten on the priority list.

For instance, will friends come before family? Will seeing friends be a regular part of every weekend or just a few times a month? What about during the week? Some people prefer to stay close to home and get their rest for work the next day rather than go out and visit with friends until late in the evening (this gets to be more the case as you age, trust me). And while it may have been fine once upon a time for your husband's friends to drop in at three o'clock in the morning, crash at his apartment, and stay for breakfast, that may not be appropriate now.

It is important to agree on the role that friends will play in your marriage and your life. Just like the ground rules set for family, you need to set some rules in the friend category as well.

The first step in deciding what role friends will play in your relationship is understanding how each partner feels about his or her friends. And the first step toward that understanding is communication. Below are some problems with friends that often come up during the first year of marriage. Use them as a guide to steer your discussion and negotiation.

- **"My husband's friends are taking him away from me. He'd rather be with them than with me."**

  This is a time issue more than anything else. Begin a dialogue with questions: Is your spouse going out with friends more or less frequently than he or she did before you were married? If the amount of time is the same, did you agree that it would change once your got married? Or did you simply expect that it would? Unspoken expectations can get newlyweds into a great deal of trouble, because one spouse has no way of knowing what the other spouse expects, or why.

Next, get to the assumptions—namely, that going out with friends is somehow a reflection on the way your mate feels about you. There are some emotional issues in these assumptions, such as the wife's feeling that her husband doesn't want to be with her, or would rather be with his friends. This really has more to do with something missing from the relationship than with the husband's friends. It should be addressed separately.

It may be that the wife in this instance had made plans for the evening, so she felt hurt and taken advantage of when the husband chose being with his friends over being with her. But did he know about her plans? Had she asked him ahead of time?

Clearly, this couple has many potential issues to resolve. If you or your mate feels this way about the other going out, the two of you need to sit down and discuss what is bothering you, openly and honestly. If it's jealousy, say so. If it's resentment at one spouse having more fun, that's something else entirely. And if it's just a matter of one partner feeling a little neglected, that can easily be solved by planning some time together. Designate Tuesday night as friends night out, for example, and reserve Saturday nights for the two of you to go out together.

- **"After we get home from work, my wife talks on the phone for hours with her friends. When she finally gets off the phone she complains that we never do anything together."**

  Again, this is primarily a time issue. It's dangerous to consider all couple time sacred, a precious resource that should not be encroached upon under any circumstance, for in doing so you'll start to resent anything or anyone that interrupts that time.

  Relax. It sounds like both partners want to spend quality time together but may be feeling pressured to do so. Don't try to cram couple time in between *Star Trek* episodes. Plan some outings, away from the phone and distractions from the rest of the world.

- **"I hate my wife's best friend."**

  This is potentially a touchy issue. By hating your spouse's best friend, particularly if that friend is a big part of your mate's life, you could be in for a battle. Of course, you could always answer the phone, "Honey, that gas-ridden, butt-dragging, genetic misfire of a friend of yours is on the phone again," although I wouldn't recommend it.

  In such cases, there are usually two issues. One is the friend issue; the other is a time issue. We've already discussed the importance of setting aside quality couple time, which should ease competition for a spouse's attention. As for the friend issue, you may inherit friends like you inherit family, but your responsibilities to your inherited friends are not as rigid as your responsibilities to your in-laws. Generally, you don't have to see your mate's friends for Thanksgiving, for example, and at your sister-in-law's graduation.

  You don't have to like your mate's best friend. It's not required. What is required is for you to leave their relationship alone. Don't try to sway your spouse against his or her best friend; you will only end up being resented. By interfering in the relationship, you'll threaten something that's valuable to your spouse, which doesn't make you look very good in the long run. Your mate will likely question your depth, or intellect, or whatever skill you are lacking that does not allow you to see all the wonderful qualities that his or her best friend has.

  The only time you should get involved in a mate's relationship with a friend is when you are concerned about his or her welfare. If that friend is a bad influence on your spouse, say, encouraging drug use heavy drinking, it may be a good idea for you to intervene. But only offer to help. Point out the pattern and voice your concern. Do not badmouth your spouse's friend, and do not issue an ultimatum, or you may be the one who ends up losing.

- **"Her friends are always here. They come Friday night and don't leave until Sunday!"**

  On an obvious level, this is a struggle for basic living space. Your home belongs to both of you, and you must both be allowed to feel comfortable in it. Friends can't be allowed to wear out their welcome with your spouse. The great weekend movie marathons may have to be curtailed to an overnight every once in a while, or stopped altogether.

On another level, the husband in this case may be expressing a desire to spend more time alone with his wife. Or he may feel he can't relax and really be himself while his wife's friends are around. His wife might help him feel more at ease if she included him in conversations and activities with her friends. Scheduling alone time together might also help.

- **"When I married my husband, I never knew I'd be marrying his friends, too."**

This situation may be more than a matter of friends wearing out their welcome. There is probably a close attachment between the husband and his friends, a bond that has been there a long time. The wife has probably had plenty of time to get used to it, so the question becomes, why does she expect it should change now?

Whatever the answer to that question, there are some ways to get around chronic friend syndrome. Again, never try to come between your mate and a gang of friends. Nine times out of ten, you will come out the loser. Instead, schedule activities with your mate that can't be changed or canceled when the gang decides at the last minute to go down to the pool hall they've been hanging out at for the last twelve years. Consult your spouse about the outing beforehand, then remind him or her as the date approaches. That way, there will be no surprises, and your mate's friends will have had time to get used to the idea.

Another option is to make plans by yourself or spend some time with your friends while your spouse spends time with his or hers. Doing things separately can provide a healthy break and even make the time you spend together more special.

- **"I'm tired of going out with your friends. When are we going to spend time with mine?"**

A tug-of-war of friends arises when both spouses have close, longstanding friendships that they want to involve their spouses in. Often a core group of friends will marry and bring their spouses into the group, making a group of couple friends. The conflict comes in when both spouses have such groups of friends. Then, with demands of work and family, time becomes a factor.

To solve this problem all you have to do is to be fair. If you want your wife with you when you go out with your friends, it's only fair that you go out with hers. If two events coincide, either go to the events separately or take turns attending events together ("We hung out with your friends for the last two weekends").

Old Flames

Past romances pose a bit of a conundrum for many newlyweds, particularly if that person is still involved in a spouse's life. While one person may be comfortable with such a relationship, another may not. It all depends on your mate. And hanging the label "insecurity" over his or her head is probably not the best action to take.

There are several scenarios that can occur with past flames:

- **Memories.** It's a long held theory that there will always be one great love in a life. If you're lucky, you married that person. But if your first love is only a fading memory, a fond recollection of your summer together in Europe, or your first semester in a college dorm, even though the individual may be long gone, you hold on. You know it didn't work out, and you're sure it couldn't have worked out, but you still think about him or her every now and again.

  Often in these cases, the memory may not be about that individual as much as it may be a longing for that time and place, or even the intensity of emotion you shared. Memories of past relationships are usually harmless—unless it disturbs your spouse. Or, unless you have elevated it from your memory to a place of desire.

- **Torch carrying.** If you're still carrying a torch for the love of your life, who is not your current spouse, you may be in for a problem. I don't know of many people who wouldn't be bothered by their husband or wife harboring romantic feelings for someone else, even if that person were far away or a childhood sweetheart. If that person is not so far away—if he or she works in the same building downtown, for example—and you find yourself daydreaming about past or future trysts, you're really in for a problem—a problem that could wreck your marriage.

- **Just friends.** Remaining friends with a past flame is not uncommon, whether the flame was the love of your life, or simply someone you were involved with at one time. Particularly if you hung around with a large group of friends and dated more than one of them. Jealousies may flare in a marriage, though, if one spouse believes there is still a spark left. The best course of action is to talk about the friendship and involve your spouse in such a way as to reduce his or her level of insecurity as much as possible. If the relationship is still a problem, there may be deeper issues to address.
- **More than friends.** Every once in a while, an old flame hangs around, still desirous of your attention and time. This is a one-sided friendship, and even if you're not willing to look at it honestly, your spouse is likely to hold you responsible, claiming that you're leading the person on. Because the recipient of such adoration is usually flattered, if not tempted to reciprocate, he or she may not want to make the other person go away. But to be fair and respectful of your spouse, that is really the only responsible action to take.

The Gender Dilemma

Some people believe, as Billy Crystal stated in *When Harry Met Sally,* that it is impossible to be close friends with someone of the opposite sex "because the sex part always gets in the way." But there are people who have close, close friends of the opposite sex and have never felt an attraction for them. I'm not talking here about relationships where one friend feels an attraction but the other does not; I'm referring to purely platonic relationships only.

In such cases, there is really no cause for jealousy, and as in the case of remaining good friends with a past girlfriend or boyfriend, spouses should be included to ease any insecurity or doubts about the harmlessness of the relationship.

The Good Side

WHATEVER YOUR dilemma with finding time to fit the rest of the world into your marriage, there is one thing for which you and your spouse should be thankful: Count yourselves lucky that you have a loving family and good friends that want to be part of your life in the first place.

Resources

Arnstein, Helene S. *Between Mothers-in-Law & Daughters-in-Law: Achieving a Successful and Caring Relationship.* New York: Dodd, Mead & Company, 1985.

Friel, John, Ph.D., and Linda Friel, M.A. *An Adult Child's Guide to What's Normal.* Deerfield Beach, Florida: Health Communications, 1990.

Horsley, Gloria. *The In-Law Survival Manual.* New York: John Wiley & Sons, 1997.

Miller, Stuart. *Men and Friendship.* Los Angeles: Jeremy P. Tarcher, 1992.

Secunda, Victoria. *Women and Their Fathers.* New York: Delta Books, 1992.

✣ BUDGETING ✣

Never ask of money spent
Where the spender thinks it went.
Nobody was ever meant
To remember or invent
What he did with every cent.
　　　　　　　　　—*Robert Frost,* The Hardship of Accounting

Money—now, that's the fun stuff. Surely, money will play only a small role in your marriage. After all, "love is all you need." Wrong. Money is the cause of more worry and more fights than practically anything else in this country. Money is what people work so hard for. It is the thing they come home with on Friday and wonder where it went by Sunday.

Now that you're married, your finances are more important than when you were single. Then, if you were late on a payment or bounced a check occasionally, you only hurt yourself. But now, you have a partner. Whatever you do with your money affects your spouse.

This and the next three chapters are about money: budgeting, credit and debt, buying a home, and investments and taxes. They will show you how to pay off everything you owe and be able to live off your investments in just a few years. By showing you how to live off your investments, I'm not saying your goal should be to quit your job, sleep until noon, watch reruns of *I Dream of Jeannie,* and then loaf around until it's time to go to bed—although some days that may sound like a lot of fun. The goal is to be financially secure, protected in the event something bad happens. What if you and your spouse both lost your jobs today? Or, from another perspective, imagine having more options: looking for a new job with a clear, confident head, opening your own business, going back to school.

The journey toward financial security begins with budgeting. Budgets provide a visual representation of where your money is going. And they can save you a great deal of money if you stick to them. If you are not currently using a budget, you're probably spending about 30 percent more than you have to. Think about that. At the end of the year someone handing you a check for 30 percent of your yearly family income. Sound interesting?

Financial advisors say that 96 percent of people in this country live from paycheck to paycheck and will not be financially independent by the time they reach retirement age. Don't be in that majority. Start building financial independence now for a secure future later. With responsible and sound financial management, you can survive the loss of your income by living off the interest generated by your investment portfolio—without ever touching the principal! That's the kind of freedom and security most people only dream of.

Yeah, so what if you don't have a million dollars to invest? What if you can barely swing $10 a week? First of all, it's important to know that the investing strategies presented here are safe and solid. Second, a sound investment package is possible with your present income. Few people realize the financial power that is within their reach. They drive late-model cars, they pay high credit card payments every month, they have thousands in student loans to pay off, they live in small apartments.

Let's take a specific example. Say you got married when you were twenty-eight years old and your combined gross family income is $32,000. And let's say that you have no drive or ability whatsoever, and will never get a raise or a better job or advance yourself in any way for the rest of your life: at the age of sixty-two you will still be making $32,000.

In that period of time, thirty-four years, to be exact, you will generate almost $1.1 million. Pretty impressive, huh?

Of course, you do have drive and ability, and you will probably get a raise or a better job at some point in your life, or at least your spouse might, so that number will more likely be closer to $2 million or even

$3 million. Let's see what you can do with that much income....

Family Income

IT'S IMPORTANT to think of your and your spouse's incomes in combined terms, as one family income. You have a partner now and, therefore, twice the financial power to wield. If you haven't done it yet, sit down and calculate your gross family income and net family income, in both monthly and yearly terms. Gross is the amount of money you make before any taxes, insurance premiums, and retirement contributions are taken out; net is the amount after those deductions. You'll need the gross income figure for filing taxes and buying a home, and the net figure to figure out your monthly budget.

Family Expenses

TO KEEP TRACK of expenses, it is often helpful to separate them into categories. There are three categories of expenses: fixed, variable, and periodic.

1. Fixed expenses are the same each month (rent, car payment).

2. Variable expenses fluctuate from month to month (groceries, gasoline, entertainment).

3. Periodic expenses occur annually, semiannually, quarterly, and so forth (insurance premium, property taxes).

A Budget Example

YOU SIT DOWN at the table on a Sunday morning, preferably not during football season when you're bound to be interrupted ("Honey, the game is on"). You've got your checkbook, bank statements, credit card statements, pens, pencils, tablets, and a pot of coffee. You're ready to try this budget thing.

You start with your income. Money coming in is always less depressing than money going out. For this example, let's say your net family income, the combined income after taxes, 401(k) contributions, and other pre-tax deductions are taken out, is $2,000 a month.

Now, you add up your monthly expenses. You begin with your fixed costs, like rent and car payments, then move on to variable costs such as groceries, utility bills, credit card payments, and so on. You do your periodic payments, such as insurance, last, and break them down into monthly amounts. Breaking periodic expenses down to monthly amounts does not mean you must pay them this way; it simply is a way to assess your costs on an even playing field. If all your other expenses are monthly, but one bill is paid every forty-two days, budgeting for that bill can get confusing.

You figure your monthly expenses as follows:

Rent	$450
Car payments (for two cars)	$410 ($230 + $180)
Savings	$100
Student loan	$75
Cable	$22
Utilities	$120
Credit cards	$100
Groceries	$180
Gas	$120
Entertainment	$200
Car insurance	$127
Left over	$96

Notice that your car insurance is only $127 a month. That's because it represents the semi-annual premium, $762, divided by six.

Once you sit down and put your budget on paper, you discover that you should have extra money at the end of every month. But, as you soon discover when you actually try to balance your checkbook at the end of the month, a budget has a sick sense of humor.

Most couples end up with a substantial amount of cash left over when they do their first budget. They jump up from the table and rummage through their stack of catalogs—they have an extra $300 a month to play with, and they're going to find something to spend it on. Trouble is, a month later they look in their checkbook and are perplexed to find not only that nothing is left over, but that some of the bills didn't even get paid that month. Where did it all go?

The answer is simple: the budget has a leak. Money is being

sucked out somehow, somewhere. At this point, budget novices will do one of two things: (1) give up the ghost and go back to unsupervised spending, or (2) sit back down at the kitchen table and try to figure out where their initial budget went awry, then give up in frustration. They cannot even make a simple budget work, they conclude, so why try anymore.

What they ought to do is find the hole and plug it.

Inspector Budget

TRACKING A BUDGET meticulously (otherwise known as "nickel and diming it"), takes a little bit of persistence and a lot of attention to detail. Invest in a couple of inexpensive notebooks—try Disney theme notebooks for fun: *101 Dalmatians, The Lion King, Pocahontas*—small tablets that you can carry around to write down everything you spend money on during the next month. Keep it in your wallet, so that every time you grab for the green you're reminded to jot it down. Don't try to change the way you spend just yet; simply go through the next thirty days as you normally would but document everything you spend. Everything. Every cup of coffee and lottery ticket, every lunch out, every newspaper, every gallon of gasoline, every package of breath mints—everything. (Well, you can probably skip the gumball you bought with the penny you found in the parking lot.) This exercise is not to punish you or make you feel guilty about the money you're spending; it's to give you an accurate profile of where your money is going.

At the end of the month sit down with both of your notebooks and add your numbers together. Make common categories such as lunches, gas, newspapers, dry cleaning, and so on.

Now go back and fill in your budget. Returning to the example above, let's say your actual expenses look like this:

Rent	$450
Car payments (for two cars)	$410 ($230 + $180)
Savings	$35
Student loan	$75
Cable	$22
Utilities	$76

Credit cards	$100
Groceries	$150
Gas	$120
Entertainment	$165
Car insurance	$127
Dry Cleaning	$35
Meals out	$235

(including lunches, treats, candy)

By the end of the month, you're actually having to dip into the $100 you put into savings at the beginning. Look at your actual expenses. If you each eat lunch out every day, you could be spending $200 a month or more just on lunches. Think about what you could do with an extra $200 a month. Or if you each buy a cup of coffee for the morning commute, that's $40 a month, just for coffee. Now, that may not seem like much, but in a year it adds up to $480. That's a full rent payment plus some extra money to apply to credit card debt!

Certainly, life should not be lived without any material comforts, including occasional treats and flamboyant purchases. You shouldn't have to eat a bologna sandwich at your desk every day and never go out to lunch again. If you want to put away $200 each month for lunch, that's your prerogative. Just realize where your money is going and make a conscious decision to spend it on lunches out. For your budget to work, you must be honest about where you're spending your money.

A Working Budget

EIGHT OUT of every ten people who try to budget become frustrated and give up. But what these 80 percent don't realize is that you have to test a budget two or three times before you get it to work.

In engineering this is known as a beta test. Engineers know that after doing all the research, all the lab work, and all the revisions, their designs still probably won't work. They need to get their idea out in the real world and see where the bugs are. Only then can they document those bugs and fix them.

At the end of your first month, the month spent with notebook in hand, you'll go through your own beta test. Did you have the money left over you thought you would? Did you get to make a double credit card payment or put extra money on the car loan like you thought you would?

More than likely, the answer will be no. But you're now armed with the information you need—namely, your true spending habits—to revise your budget and try again. Three is usually the magic number for budget revisions. But don't give up if it takes four or five. Once you get a solid working budget, budgeting will pay off in only a few months. Once you know where your money is going, you can find those areas where savings can be realized.

Finding Ways to Save

Most people can cut a significant portion from their entertainment and dining expenses with no hardship at all. Finding low-cost ways of entertaining yourself is an excellent first step. Rather than going out for a drink at a bar, for example, pick up a bottle of wine at the liquor store and stay home. Instead of going to a movie theater Saturday night, try renting a video from the local video store—you can rent four videos for the price of two adult movie tickets on a weekend night, and that's not even including the popcorn. If this isn't practical—say you've already seen every video released since 1955—try going to a matinee instead of a full-price show. If you go out to a movie and dinner once a week, limit the number of times you go to an expensive restaurant to once or twice a month. On alternate weeks get pizza, or go to a family restaurant where prices are more reasonable. Ways to save money are only as limited as your imagination.

Once you've reduced your flexible spending, it's time to lower the cost of necessities—telephone expenses, for instance. Long-distance telephone costs can be reduced by shopping around for the best plan—with the competition between the big three, Sprint, MCI, and AT&T, there are good deals out there—as well as calling during off-peak hours. Taking turns calling relatives—you call Grandma one week and she calls you the next—can reduce your costs sharply. Besides, grandmas usually don't mind sharing part of this expense. Or you can always practice that dying art—letter writing. For couples with computers at home, E-mail provides a low-cost alternative to high telephone bills. You're paying the monthly charge anyway; you may as well use the free transmission time you're paying for.

Utility costs, too, can be easily reduced by investing in energy-efficient appliances and fixtures, adjusting your thermostat, using water aerators on showers and faucets, and keeping your refrigerator and air conditioner clean and in efficient working condition. In fact, by taking a few simple, low-cost steps, you can reduce your total energy usage, and cost, by as much as 50 percent, depending upon your efficiency rating now. Contact your local utility company for tips on increasing your energy efficiency. Many utility companies offer free energy audits.

Grocery shopping has gotten to be an expensive undertaking, to say the least. Food manufacturers have invested millions, probably billions, in getting people to buy and stay loyal to their brands. And that's not all that's working against you. As you steer your cart through each aisle at the grocery store, products are carefully arranged so that the more expensive items are at eye level, leaving the cheaper, generic brands to the shelves just out of reach. Package sizing, too, makes a difference in the price you pay for certain foods. Soup, for example, comes in single servings as well as family servings. The price per ounce for the larger sizes can be much less than the smaller sizes, meaning you're paying for the can and the convenience of not having leftovers.

All is not lost, however. You don't need a degree in marketing or economics to save money at the grocery store. By using the following tips, you should be able to cut your grocery bill substantially.

- **Cut coupons.** You can save up to 30 percent by using manufacturer and store coupons. In just a few minutes—fifteen, if you chew out the coupons with your teeth rather than cut them out with scissors—you could save as much as $25 a month. That's $60 an hour for your trouble!
- **Shop on days that stores offer double coupons.**
- **Stockpile.** When your local grocer has tuna on sale for thirty-one cents a can, buy a few dollars' worth and use that until it goes on sale the next time (best not use this strategy on fresh food—not much is saved if you're throwing out half of what you buy).
- **Use rebates.** Many people are sucked into buying a product by

the rebate price, but never get around to sending in the rebate, so they end up giving money to the manufacturer. Like coupons, just a few minutes of effort can pay off big.

- **Save manufacturer coupons until your grocer has that item on sale. Then stockpile.**
- **Never go shopping hungry.** It's something your mom probably told you, but it's true. Everything looks good when you're hungry, especially those expensive deli and bakery items.
- **Stick to a list.** Make a list of what you need, and unless something is on sale and worth stockpiling, or unless you forgot something that you genuinely need—that pitcher-style Tupperware cereal dispenser and those kitchen towels with the duckies on them don't count—stick to your list.
- **Buy generic products.** They typically cost 20 percent less than the name brands.
- **Buy in bulk.** It's not just soup companies that make money on smaller, "more convenient," single-serving sizes. But be careful, you don't always save with the larger size, either.
- **Plan meals ahead of time.** You're more likely to stick to your list, and you won't end up throwing away vegetables and other assorted produce that you bought because you thought you'd eat it but never got around to preparing it.
- **Make bigger meals and take leftovers for lunch.** One of the main reasons people don't bring their lunches to work is because a cold sandwich doesn't always hit the spot, especially on a cold, snowy, dreary day at the office. Heating up that yummy casserole—now, that's a different story. You'll probably start feeling hungry for lunch by the time your first coffee break rolls around.

A Debt-Reduction Budget

The bottom line on budgets is, they are designed to help you meet your financial goals. And whatever those goals, there is a budget that will accomplish it.

Let's say you go out and buy $2,000 worth of furniture. It's great fun to whip out that plastic and sign for it, but you may feel differently when the time comes to pay if off. So you decide to finance the payments over a longer period of time. "No problem," you say to yourself when you see that low minimum monthly payment of $33.09. But paying only the minimum amount due each month, it would take almost thirty years to pay off the original balance of $2,000, and with interest you'd end up paying a total of almost $12,000! That's five times the original principal amount just for interest. Clearly, reducing your debt, creating a cash reserve, and making your money work for you is a better option.

A debt-reduction budget is one that whittles away a particular debt with all the extra cash you have. When that debt is paid off, you move onto the next, using the money you'd normally spend for the debt you just paid off as well as your extra cash. You continue to whittle your debt away until eventually you're debt-free.

Using the previous budget as an example, after some money-saving strategies were implemented in the areas of entertainment and lunches out, your debt-reduction budget would look like the following:

Net monthly income	$2000
Debt Expenses	
Credit cards	$325
Car payments (for two cars)	$410 ($230 + $180)
Student loan	$75
Other expenses	
Rent	$450
Savings	$0
Cable	$22
Utilities	$76
Groceries	$150
Gas	$120
Entertainment	$75
Car insurance	$127
Dry Cleaning	$35
Meals out	$135
(including lunches, treats, candy)	

In this example, you choose to reduce your credit card debt by using all the money you were putting into savings, including the $190 you saved on eating out and entertaining, to pay off your credit cards. (Grocery expense remains constant, because any savings are offset by the additional cost of groceries for lunches.) After all, what's the use in earning 2 percent interest on the money in your savings account if you're paying 18 percent interest on your credit cards? When the credit cards are paid off, you will take that $325 and add it to the car payment to pay the first car off. When that car is paid off, you will take the $505 and add it to the car payment to pay the second car off.

Within ten months, you will have your credit cards and both cars paid off completely, but only if you do not take on additional debt. After that ten months you will have an extra $735 a month to invest. Notice that you choose to keep the student loan as a debt. Even though student loans do fall under the category of debt in a technical sense, the interest is usually low enough that it is worth it to pay off the loan over the full term.

Now comes the fun part…. You take that $735 a month and put it into an investment program for one year. With a 15 percent rate of return, that money—the same money that was going toward interest and getting you nothing—will be worth almost $9,500!

The intricacies and strategies of investing will be discussed later; this is just a teaser to get you thinking about what your money could be doing for you instead of someone else.

Living Off One Paycheck

YEARS AGO, most families lived on only one paycheck. The man went out and earned the living while the woman stayed at home and raised the kids. Well, believe it or not, that lifestyle is gaining popularity once again. Only this time around, the paycheck does not necessarily come from the man. Simplifying, scaling back—these are sentiments among many baby boomers today, and even many Generation X-ers, who have figured out that trading your life for a paycheck isn't all it's cracked up to be.

Let's say that someday—maybe not today or tomorrow, but someday—you plan on having a family. Your financial goal, then, is to get out of debt, and slowly shift all the financial responsibilities from two paychecks to one, until you are able to live on one check and put the other into an investment program.

There are two great advantages to doing this: first, you'll be putting large chunks of money away, that will create large returns relatively quickly. For example, investing a monthly paycheck of $850 will build to $23,000 in as little as two years. Second, living off one check gives one or the other spouse the freedom to choose to stay home with a child. Or, maybe to work part-time. Or start a small home-based business. The point is, you'll have options.

Electronic Budgeting

IF YOU DON'T trust your mind or your math skills to do all this high finance stuff, there is a great deal of budgeting software on the market today. Intuit's Quicken dominates the home-budgeting software world, with Microsoft's Money running a close second. Quicken sells for between $19.95 and $100 ($39 is the average), and is available in Windows or Macintosh. It does everything for you, short of going to the store: It can balance a checkbook, track a budget, monitor investments and savings, and produce colorful graphs and charts that show you at a glance where you will be financially in the years to come. It's latest version, Quicken 6.0, offers the option of paying your bills and doing your banking on-line. Plus, someone with absolutely no understanding of accounting can use it effectively (in this case, I'd recommend taking the tutorial to get started).

Microsoft's Money software does everything Quicken does, but has some advantages overall. For example, switching to different screens is easier in Money than in Quicken, and the financial calculators in Money are more advanced, offering the capability of adding amounts to monthly loan payments to see how much interest you can save; setting a savings goal and seeing how long it will take you to reach it, with varying interest rates and monthly contributions; and amortizing mortgage and other debt payments for faster payoffs. Money runs around $30 or less.

Cash Graph Incorporated has come up with a unique approach to budgeting software. Rather than offering customers useless or frivolous extras, Cash Graph sells three separate software packages, each of which focuses on a specific aspect of home budgeting. There is

Cash Graph Checking for basic budgeting and bills; Cash Graph Personal Inventory for investments, savings, and other financial goals; and Cash Graph Appointment for time management. Each package runs around $10.

The advantage to budgeting electronically is the accuracy and convenience of having all your financial information and history at your fingertips, when you need it, with very little effort. Particularly at tax time each year. Quicken, like other accounting packages, keeps track of tax-related accounts and can generate reports that tell you which totals go where on what form. And if you update your version every year, which is usually less expensive than buying a new package, you can do your own taxes. Quicken even prints out the forms. All you have to do is enter your account and checkbook information. The program does the rest. Of course, using accounting software does require some maintenance time to keep your financial records entered and up-to-date in the computer, but for the time you'll save at the end of the year, it is well worth it.

Resources

Cut Your Bills in Half, by the Editors of Rodale Press. Emmaus, Pennsylvania: Rodale Press, 1989.

Scott, David L. *The Guide to Personal Budgeting.* Old Saybrook, Connecticut: The Globe Pequot Press, 1992.

Dominguez, Joe and Vicki Robin. *Your Money or Your Life.* New York: Viking, 1992.

CREDIT AND DEBT

A creditor is worse than a master, for a master owns only your person;
a creditor owns your dignity, and can belabor that.

—*Victor Hugo,* Les Miserables

It's a catch-22: people must first establish credit to get credit, so they can go into debt; they can't get credit if they're in debt, however, because being in debt is bad, even though having debt is necessary to establish good credit which is good. So they go into debt to establish their credit and end up with bad credit because they couldn't handle their debt.

Huh?

Here's a simple way to look at it. As much as 40 percent of your paycheck goes to Uncle Sam. For the average person, another third goes to interest and debt. That means most people live on less than a third of their income, more specifically, they have 26 percent to buy food and clothing, to invest, to spend on vacations, to raise families, to retire on.

But what if you could get out of debt, or avoid debt completely, invest your money, and live off the interest from your investments? And what if you could do it in a relatively short period of time?

Option 1: The Cash Method

THINK ABOUT IT. If you were out of debt and owned your home outright, the amount of money you'd need to live on would be a fraction of what it is now. You would only need enough money to cover the basics: food, clothing, gasoline, utilities, and, of course, taxes. Returning to the example from the previous chapter, you would need $815 a month to live on, or only $9,780 a year. And you would be able to live the same lifestyle you're living now. Even better, you could be earning that money without working.

To generate enough money to live on without having to work, you need an investment large enough to earn your required income in interest. To calculate the size of that investment, divide the amount of money you need to live on each month by .008. The couple above, for example, would need $101,875 in their investment plan to net $815 a month in interest.

While it may seem that it would take a lifetime to acquire so much money, using only your present income (meaning no promotions or salary increases), you could do it in less than eight years if you invested $735 a month at, say, 12 percent interest. Theoretically, you could retire at a very young age. The point is that just because you weren't born with money doesn't mean you can't be financially independent.

Let's try another example using the cash method, this time factoring in buying and paying for a house. Your net income once again will be $2,000. Within the constraints of this income, you want to use cash to buy a used car to replace the one you have. Your second car will last another few years but will definitely need to be replaced then. You also want to begin saving for a down payment on a house.

Buying cars with cash? Come on! This may seem unrealistic at first glance. After all, if people could pay for cars with cash, why would anyone choose to pay any interest at all? And how do you pay for something with cash when you have nothing in the bank? The answer lies in making your money work for you. The more money you invest, the more money you make.

Let's take your goals, one at a time.

1. A used car, as soon as possible

   Cost: $7,000

If you can hold onto your car a little longer by carpooling or even sharing a car, in just under ten months you could buy a replacement vehicle with cash. (Investing $735 a month at 12 percent interest in ten months would yield $7,689.73.) What's more, that ten months of inconvenience would save you the interest portion of a four-year loan at 10 percent (a typical loan rate and period for a used car), or $1,522, which is nearly 22 percent of the cost of another car. By waiting, you will be more than one-fifth of the way to being able to afford your next car, which is goal number two.

2. A second used car, as soon as possible

Cost: $7,000

In another ten months after purchasing your first car, you now can afford to pay for a second one in cash, saving another $1,522. That means, in just over a year and a half you have purchased two cars and saved $3,044 in interest payments. If you had financed both cars, you would have been paying them off for up to eight years. By paying in cash, you can start saving for your house more than six years earlier than if you'd bought the cars on credit.

3. A house, as soon possible

Cost: $60,000

In the second year, after the twenty months it has taken to buy both cars, you can begin saving for a house. Investing $735 a month at 12 percent interest, you will have saved enough to pay cash for the house, and have $11,576 left over for decorating, in only six years! In less than eight years—seven years and eight months, to be exact—you will have paid for two cars and a new home in cash.

Let's take this example through to retirement age. Suppose you took the full four years to pay off each car, and spent all your extra cash over those eight years. It would take two more years just to save the down payment on a home. If you got a typical thirty-year mortgage at 9 percent interest, at the end of forty years you'd have a home and, assuming you invested the difference between that $735 extra a month and your mortgage payment during those thirty years, a sizeable nest egg to show for it. (Let's assume for simplicity's sake that the two cars last thirty years.) Investing $300 a month ($735 minus a $435 mortgage payment) will yield $868,798 in thirty years. Sounds impressive, doesn't it?

Using the cash method, however, you would be able to save enough to buy both cars and the house in less than eight years, and would then have $1185 a month ($735 plus the $450 used for rent) to invest for the remaining thirty-two years. Your nest egg would be substantially larger, a whopping $4.33 million.

This is all on paper, of course. It does not take into account inflation or other financial factors that may come into play over the next thirty years. But it also assumes your income will remain fixed and never increase, so the figures in this example could turn out to be conservative.

Year	Cash Method	Credit Method
Year 1	Buy first car in cash; cost: $7,000	Take out first car loan
Year 2	Buy second car in cash; cost: $7,000	
Year 4		Pay off first car; cost: $8,522; take out second car loan
Year 8	Buy house in cash; cost: $60,000	Pay off second car; cost: $8,522
Year 10		Down payment for house saved; cost: $6,000 (10% of $60,000); take out thirty-year mortgage ($54,000)
Year 40		House paid off; cost: $156,420
Assets	$74,000	$74,000
Costs	$74,000	$179,464
Time	8 years	40 years
Nest egg	$4.33 million	$868,798

Option 2: The Credit/Cash Method

WHILE IT LOOKS great on paper, the cash method may not always be practical; using a combination of cash and credit may be more feasible for many people. With this type of plan, the goal is to go into debt but get out as quickly as possible. The advantage over cash is that you can buy the items you want sooner, and then pay them off before incurring more debt. To illustrate, let's use the same income and expense scenario as above, with the same three goals.

1. A used car, as soon as possible

   Cost. $7,000

   You would like to wait until you could pay cash, but there's no way your car will last ten months. Let's assume you can finance the entire amount, and you take out a loan at 10 percent interest. (Interest rates on used car loans vary from state to state, and from year to year. Typically, the interest rate charged for a used car is higher than that charged for a new car.) If you make regular payments, it will take you four years to pay for your used car and you will have paid a total of $8,522 for it. Your monthly car payment will be $177.54 a month.

   A certain portion of each payment goes toward interest and the rest toward the principal. Most payment plans have the interest loaded on the front, so in the beginning of a loan more than half of the monthly payment is interest. To keep it simple, let's use the average interest charged over the life of the loan—in this case $1,522 divided by 4 divided by 12—or $37.71 a month. That means $139.83 of every payment goes to pay off the principal.

   You have $735 a month to spend. If you apply that entire $735 toward you car loan each month, $697 would go towards the principal ($735 minus $38 interest a month). At that rate, the car would be paid off in eleven months, which would be only one month longer than if you had saved for ten months and paid for the car in cash. By paying the loan off early, though, you will be responsible for only $349 in interest charges—a savings of $1173 in interest, assuming there are no prepayment penalties charged by the lender.

   The same goes for the second car. If you take out a second car loan the next year and pay for it using the same method, you will only get into one debt situation at a time and save quite a bit in interest by paying it off early.

2. A home, as soon as you can afford it

Cost: $60,000

After paying off both car loans in just about two years and putting your extra money into an investment plan, you have saved enough money for a down payment by the end of the third year (so we'll say the beginning of the fourth year to keep it simple). Now you can take out a thirty-year mortgage. With a 9 percent loan, your mortgage payment will be $434.50. Using the simplified average-interest calculation used above, the amount that goes toward the principal each month is only $150; the remaining $285 goes to interest.

Applying the full $735 toward your monthly mortgage payment, as well as the amount you had paid for rent ($450), a full $901 would go toward the principal each month, which would enable you to pay off your mortgage in five years. What's more, you would pay a mere $17,100 in interest, as opposed to the $102,420 you would have had to pay over thirty years.

If you then invested the amount you had been paying toward your mortgage and interest ($1185), in the remaining thirty-one years your nest egg would be $3.86 million.

You can compare all three methods in tabular form on the following page.

Digging Out

THESE TWO METHODS work well, for those who can pinch some extra money out of the budgets each month. But what if you're already so far in debt that you have no extra money to make extra payments?

You go back through your budget. As explained in the last chapter, there are numerous ways to save money. If your budget happens to be tighter than the one used in the previous examples, you'll just have to start smaller, that's all. For example, maybe you already bring your lunch three times a week, so spending for lunches totals only $80 a month. Start there. By purchasing less expensive lunch food and bringing your lunch four days a week, you'll have an extra $40 a month to start to pay off your credit card. Then, once your credit card

Year	Cash Method	Credit Method	Credit/Cash Method
Year 1	Buy first car in cash; cost: $7,000	Take out first car loan	Take out first car loan; pay off first car loan; cost: $7,349
Year 2	Buy second car in cash;cost: $7,000		Take out second car loan; pay off second car loan; cost $7,349
Year 4		Pay off first car; cost: $8,522; take out second car loan	Down payment for house saved; cost $6,000 (10% of $60,000); take out thirty-year mortgage ($54,000)
Year 8	Buy house in cash; cost: $60,000	Pay off second car; cost: $8,522	
Year 9			House paid off; cost $71,100
Year 10		Down payment for house saved; cost: $6,000 (10% of $60,000); take out thirty-year mortgage ($54,000)	
Year 40		House paid off; cost: $156,420	
Assets	$74,000	$74,000	$74,000
Cost	$74,000	$179,464	$91,790
Time	8 years	40 years	9 years
Nest egg	$4.33 million	$868,798	$3.86 million

is paid off, you'll have that money to apply to your car payment, and so on.

Let's illustrate using a different example. Say your net family income is $1,600 a month, while your current debt and budget are as outlined below.

Debt Expenses
Credit card one	$100	(Balance = $1,080)
Credit card two	$180	(Balance = $1,260)
Car payments	$230	(Balance = $2,070)
Student loan	$75	(Balance = $4,000)

Other expenses
Rent	$450
Savings	$0
Utilities	$80
Groceries	$155
Gas	$70
Entertainment	$70
Car insurance	$90
Meals out	$100

(including lunches, treats, candy)

The first thing you need to do is analyze your debt. By looking for the balances that can be paid off the fastest, the ones that have the smallest balance left to pay, you can pay those off first and then take the money used for that debt and roll it onto the next debt.

By cutting $40 a month from meals and shaving $10 from your grocery budget, for example, you will have $50 extra to apply toward your credit card balance. And by taking $50 from the second credit card payment of $180 a month (leaving a monthly payment of $130) and applying it to the first (if they're both charging the same interest rate, the interest costs will largely balance out), you will be able to pay an extra $100 a month on the first credit card, so that bill will be paid off within six months. Next, by adding the $200 you were paying on the first credit card to the second credit card payment of $130 a month, for a total payment of $330, the second credit card account will be paid off within a couple of more months. (Another alternative would be consolidating the balances onto one low-interest credit card.) Of course, these projections assume that you won't be making anymore major purchases on your cards while you're trying to pay them off.

Now you can add $330 a month—what you were paying on your credit card accounts—onto your monthly car payment of $230, for a total of $560 a month, and pay off the car within a few more months. See how the benefits snowball? In less than a year and a half, you will have paid off all your debts except one student loan, which, as already mentioned, should be paid off over the full term of the loan. And you thought you couldn't afford any extra payments.

The Basics of Credit

NOW THAT YOU'RE out of debt, you may want to start thinking about buying a house. If you've chosen the credit/cash method outlined above, you'll need one thing to begin: good credit.

Establishing credit is really quite simple. Credit institutions are more than happy to extend credit; it is, after all, the way they make billions of dollars every year. They usually decide based on only a few criteria: past credit history, employment record, income, and sometimes outstanding debt.

If you have no credit history and are seeking a large loan, you may want to develop a credit history first. You can do this relatively quickly, simply by acquiring a department store charge card. If you've been in a mall lately, you've probably seen tables at department store entrances offering you a choice between a golf towel and a lovely pen and pencil set just for filling out a credit application. Some stores even offer a 10 percent discount off your first purchase if you apply for a store card. Get one or two of these cards, charge something, and pay off the full balance. Voila, you have a perfect credit history.

If you already have credit, but missed some payments when things got tight a while ago, you may have a poor credit rating. You should know, it's relatively easy for someone to get your credit report. The only information that's required is your address, name, and social security number. Also, federal law prohibits anyone doing a credit check on you to give you your own report. To check the status of your credit rating, you can send away for a copy of your credit report.

The credit reporting industry is dominated by three main corporations: TRW, TransUnion, and Equifax. TRW offers one free credit report a year, but remember, when you get it you are seeing only a portion of your credit history. When applying for a mortgage or other large loan, the lending agency will request a full factual file, which is a report from all three companies. Your full factual file will list all current and past debt and your payment history. In order to see your complete credit history you'll need to contact Equifax and TransUnion and request an application.

Once you receive your credit reports, the first thing to do is check them for errors. More often than not, you'll find at least one. These companies issue more than 1 million credit reports every day, and are not always timely about correcting errors and updating information.

Once you've studied your report carefully, and are confident about its accuracy, focus on your outstanding debt. If you have overdue debt, take care of that first. Contact the holder of the loan and arrange a payment schedule. Lenders of guaranteed loans for students will not settle for anything less than the full amount owed, but many banks and credit cards have been known to negotiate.

When negotiating to pay an old debt off, try to get the institution to refer to the debt as a non-rated loan on your credit report. A non-rated classification will take away the overdue status of the debt. Your report will show that no money is due, so it will be in neither good nor bad standing. If you do have any bad ratings, it will take three years for them to be taken off your credit report.

Needless to say, keeping your credit rating in good standing is very important. The most common reason people misuse their credit cards is impatience. They simply can't wait; they have to buy that something now. There are some tricks to avoid impatient spending, which are outlined below. They all require some forethought and a little self-restraint, however. Short of that, there is only one surefire road to success: Cut up that plastic.

- **Use store layaway plans instead of credit cards.** You'll pay a little at a time and have your merchandise in a few weeks. Try to find a store that has no layaway fee; that way, you pay only the ticket price for the item.

- **Avoid thinking of purchases in terms of monthly payments.** That $17 minimum payment will drag on forever, and add up fast, when $15.75 of it is interest. The way to get around this is to multiply the payments by the length of time you'll be paying them. Then ask yourself if what you're buying is really worth what you're actually going to be paying for it.
- **Whenever you happen upon one of the "must haves," stop, count to ten, and ask yourself if having it is worth delaying your retirement, or whatever you're saving for.** If you're still chanting "gimme gimme gimme" to yourself, walk away. If you still want the item enough to go back for it, then buy it with a clear conscience.
- **Keep a picture of your goal (your house, a car, a beautiful beach scene if you're saving for a vacation, whatever) in your wallet and on your mirror.** Look at it often. Remind yourself that the suffering you may feel you cannot endure a second longer is going to be worth it when you're thirty-five years old, have your house paid for, and can do whatever you want for the rest of your life.

Debt Overload: A Case History

One couple did not think they had enough self-restraint to stay out of debt. Not only did they max out their credit cards (and they had several), they also bought such big-ticket items as an in-ground pool and a boat. In only three years, not counting their home and their two cars, the couple was $65,000 in debt.

Factoring in car loans and their mortgage, they owed more then $200,000. But that's the face value of their debt, not including interest. Taking into account the accruing interest, the debt was closer to a half a million. Their family income totaled $42,000. Here's what they did:

1. They stopped using their credit cards. In a bold, and physically painful move, they cut up all their plastic. This was extremely difficult for them because they had developed a regular habit of using credit cards for everything. At first, they felt insecure and unsafe without their cards, but the feelings didn't last. They knew that it wouldn't

matter how good their plan was, it wouldn't work if they continued to build up debt.

2. They identified the amount they owed on every card, and started to pay it off, beginning with the card they owed the least amount on.

3. They gave themselves a fixed allowance, period. When it was gone, they had to wait until they got paid again. They quickly learned to make that money last.

4. They had a small portion of each paycheck deposited directly into savings for emergencies. Creating a small stockpile of cash in case something came up made them feel more secure, and it ensured that they would not have to resort to using credit for an emergency.

5. They rewarded themselves once a month for staying on the plan.

At the time of this writing, the couple had paid off five of their seven credit cards. When the last two are paid off, they will start paying off their vehicle loans. They are excited about what they have done so far and eagerly anticipate being debt free. In fact, at last contact, they said that the reduction in stress and the peace of mind that comes from knowing their financial plan is solid and they are well on their way to achieving financial independence surpasses all the fun and excitement they got out of their purchases.

Resources

Organizations

To request your free credit report from TRW, call 1-800-392-1122. To request a credit report application from Equifax, call 1-800-685-1111. The cost is $8 and processing usually takes about three weeks. To request a credit report application from TransUnion, call 1-800-922-5490. The cost is $8 and processing usually takes about three weeks.

Publications

Ambraziejus, Andrew. *Managing Credit and Credit Cards*. Stamford, Connecticut: Longmeadow Press, 1992.

Hammond, Bob. *Life Without Debt*. Franklin Lakes, New Jersey: The Career Press, 1995.

❧ BUYING A HOME ❧

Happy the man, whose wish and care
A few paternal acres bound,
Content to breathe his native air
In his own ground.

—Alexander Pope, Ode on Solitude

ccording to a 1993 *Modern Bride* survey, 53 percent of all newlyweds in this country live in a residence they own. That means more than half of the 2.5 million couples who will marry this year already own their home, or will within twelve months of marrying.

When is the right time for buying a home? Should you follow that long-honored tradition of keeping up with the Joneses and buy a home just because half of all newlyweds own their homes within the first year? The question is, are you ready to buy a house?

Case in point: more than 40 percent of houses that are repossessed belonged to couples under the age of thirty-five. So a certain number of that 53 percent bought too fast.

Buying Too Fast

IT'S EASY TO GET caught in the "next logical step" trap of buying a home. Because people expect young couples to do things in a certain order—get married, buy a house, have two-point-five children, join the local Audubon society, join a car pool, and throw a Tupperware party—many newlyweds oblige and buy a home too soon. Some may have money left over from the wedding or their parents have offered to help out, so they start looking for a house. Somehow, buying a house is deemed a sign of success, or at least of being on your way to success. Then, before you know it, you're standing on the back step gossiping with Fred about the neighbor who never seems to have wash hanging on the clothes line, or chatting with Blanche about the new Slush Boy 950 snowblower with an eight-horsepower engine and twice the throwing power of the 750.

The process of looking for a house can be a great joy, where you find "the one" serendipitously, as though it fell from the sky right in front of you. It can also be a nightmare. You search, and look, and read, and drive around neighborhoods—it can drag on for months. Either way, when you find your dream house or condo or trailer home or igloo, you know it. It feels like home.

That's when automatic pilot takes over. The whirlwind of paperwork and credit checks and income verification begins as you plod through the arduous task of applying for a mortgage, all so you can wait patiently for a phone call from the mortgage company. Will you be approved? And just why were you three days late on that credit card payment six years ago? Just when it looks like you're going to be in that apartment forever, the loan goes through, the closing date is set, and before you know it you're sitting at a big table while a seemingly motionless stream of papers flow past for you to sign, initial, and then initial that you signed. Then, it's done. You get your two sets of house keys, your briefcase-sized folder containing all the papers you just signed, and a relieved "congratulations" from everyone around the big table.

But now what? You've got a big empty house in need of a few gallons of paint, new carpet, wallpaper, linoleum that's not mustard yellow and beige, light fixtures that aren't kerosene-powered, and oh, while we're on the subject, curtains, too. And don't forget the new washer and dryer and refrigerator—this time in anything but avocado green—and the lawnmower, patio furniture, gas grill, and microwave that actually fits in the microwave cabinet.

That's when you realize you may have gotten in over your head. All of a sudden, your monthly budget looks like this:

Mortgage	$436
Hazard insurance	$19
FHA insurance	$37
Property taxes	$184
Car payments	$410
Credit cards	$285
Student loan	$75
Department store charge (washer/dryer)	$68
Car insurance	$127
Groceries	$150
Entertainment	$140
Cable	$22
Gas	$120
Monthly net expenses	$2073
Monthly net income	$2,000
Shortfall	$73

My wife and I were in no real hurry to buy a home. For starters, we weren't sure if we would be staying in the area and didn't want to be tied down should we decide to move. We also liked certain aspects of the renter-landlord relationship. Something broken? Call the land-lord. Don't like the way something looks? Call the landlord. And on those hot, sticky summer days, I'd politely ask our landlord to mow only during commercials, or at least be on the far side of the house when he passed out from heat exhaustion (those paramedics can be so noisy). We decided to settle down, however, when we realized that, over the years, we'd probably paid enough in rent for an English tutor and a summer home on Cap Cod.

For us, one of the most satisfying aspects of buying a home was doing it completely on our own. We did not have to borrow a dime from anyone. Not that borrowing is wrong; many young people bor-row the down payment from their parents or in-laws. But our ability to buy our home with no outside help was one of the reasons we knew we hadn't bought too fast. That, and the fact that we had done all the math over and over and over again, and knew we were ready financially to take on the burden of a mortgage.

One of the advantages of waiting as long as we did was catching the housing market in a slump. We paid significantly less than our house was worth and took advantage of a low interest rate. That way, we knew that unless the bottom dropped out of the local housing market entirely we would at least break even. Back in the '80s, when property values were high and getting higher every day, it didn't make sense to wait. Fortunes were made by people who bought today and sold tomorrow. Even a year or two could mean a significant gain in the value of a house. Today, however, property values have flattened. In this type of market, many home owners would lose a large chunk of money on their homes if they decided to sell.

So when is the right time to buy? Many experts claim there is a right time of year to buy a home. Fewer homes are sold in late-December and during the holidays than any other time during the year. Owners who must sell for business or personal reasons are desperate by this time, particularly if their home has been on the market all year, and will often do whatever it takes to sell. The seller's desperation is the buyer's advantage. Of course, the buyer should be wary of a house that hasn't sold for a significant length of time—there may be something wrong with it. The worst time of year to buy, according to experts, is late spring and early summer. This is peak real estate season, when kids are out of school for summer break and, in the northern half of the country at least, a move would be easiest. For most buyers, too, spring is the start of the looking season. So, while the selection is good, competition for the bargains is high and owners aren't usually as willing to negotiate.

Timing isn't limited to the month on the calendar, however. The following factors are crucial when assessing whether or not you are ready to buy a house.

You should buy your first home

1. when you can afford it. After you have fine-tuned your budget, delete your rent payment and insert your mortgage payment, including principal and interest and insurance and property taxes, plus 10 percent for emergencies (and there will be plenty of emergencies, believe me). If your budget doesn't squeal and choke and hiss, that's a good sign.

2. when you can either afford all the down payment and closing costs yourself, or can pay your family and friends back within a

year or so. If you borrow the money, add the amount you will pay back each month into your budget and see if it still works. Even if the lender is dear old Mom, budgeting to pay this money back is important: it will give you a sense of fulfillment when you make the last payment.

3. when the money you have, or are borrowing, can cover everything. Besides the obvious expenses—down payment and closing costs—other incidentals are sure to arise. Will the house need to be painted in the first year? Will you need a lawn mower, snow shovels, or lawn rakes? Do you need appliances or furniture? This isn't to say you'll need to purchase a brand new washer and dryer, along with the forty-five-cubic-foot refrigerator with ice maker and water dispenser. But planning to sleep on the floor and wash your clothes in the sink for the first year is not realistic, either.

4. when you're buying for the right reasons. Because you want a home to raise your family in, because you're ready financially, because you want to start to build equity—these are all good reasons to buy. Because all the other couples you know are buying houses, because you want to crank your stereo up without people complaining, because your class reunion is coming up and you don't want to admit you're still renting—these are not good reasons to buy.

5. when your instincts about the house or trailer or condo or igloo are good. You can do mental computations and run the what-ifs until the cows come home, but there's one additional thing you need to check out: your gut. Don't ignore what your instincts are telling you. The biggest mistakes people make are when they try to make a situation work in spite of bad feelings about it. If your gut says no, listen.

Buying Too Big

JUST BECAUSE a mortgage company approves you for a certain amount does not mean you can afford it. In fact, sometimes mortgage companies approve clients for a fairly wide range, say, somewhere between $68,000 and $79,000. It's important to remember what happened when doing your budget for the first time. You'll always look better on paper, so if it looks as though you can just swing your mortgage payments, you may be buying too big.

Because mortgage companies take such elaborate measures to approve a mortgage, many young home buyers assume that the ratio is a good one. Typically, mortgage companies go on the 30 percent rule: your debt payments, including your mortgage, insurance, and taxes, total 30 percent of your income. But what they don't tell young couples is that the mortgage company will not lose money, even if the mortgage results in a foreclosure. On a conventional mortgage, when your down payment is less than 20 percent, lenders usually charge you a higher interest rate and require you to purchase private mortgage insurance, PMI, to protect them from losses if you default on your loan. This insurance is added to your monthly rate. When you have built up 20 percent equity your mortgage payment goes down. FHA-insured and VA-guaranteed loans also protect lenders against possible borrower default by attaching additional mortgage insurance to monthly payments.

Sometimes materialism corrupts good sense, and instead of a cute little starter home you go for the four-bedroom colonial. Next thing you know, you have a huge mortgage payment, your taxes are twice what they would have been on a smaller house, and if you add in a few of the basics like a stove and refrigerator and washer and dryer, you're maxed out on all your credit cards. And you don't even have any furniture yet.

Think about your financial goals before rushing headlong into a mortgage you cannot afford. Concentrate on the long term, look at the larger picture. Start slow. Debt is okay as long as it's controllable; in other words, don't let debt control you.

The old rule of thumb was, twice your yearly salary is what you can afford in a home. Of course, that meant your net salary less your total debt. That formula is a little out of whack, however—which is probably why it's not used that often anymore—because it suggests that a single person without debt who earns $40,000 a year and a family of four with the same net income can both afford an $80,000 mortgage.

The following worksheet will help you determine how much you can afford to pay each month for your mortgage payment.

1. Calculate your total income and spending.

A. Net Monthly Family Income (after taxes and investment deductions): $ _____

Monthly Expenses, other than housing:

Food	$ _____
Renter insurance	$ _____
Medical insurance	$ _____
Medical bills not covered by insurance	$ _____
Car insurance	$ _____
Car loans	$ _____
Gasoline	$ _____
Other transportation	$ _____
Credit cards	$ _____
Other loans	$ _____
Child care	$ _____
Alimony or child support	$ _____
Clothing	$ _____
Charity	$ _____
Spending money	$ _____
(including movies, lunches, entertainment)	
Dues and subscriptions	$ _____
Other	$ _____

B. Total Expenses: $ _____

2. Calculate your maximum monthly mortgage payment.

A. Subtract your total monthly expenses from your monthly family income (A minus B): $ _____

B. Multiply by 0.9 (90%) to allow for emergency expenditures: $ _____

C. (A minus B) x 0.9 = Maximum Monthly Mortgage Payment: $ _____

A note of caution: This worksheet can be as misleading as the out-of-date rule of thumb mentioned above. The more conservative you are, the better. If it won't restrict you to living in an outhouse in someone's backyard, try to multiply the total you computed in 2A by 80 percent (.80) instead of 90 percent. At worst you'll have some extra money to stash away each month.

One young couple did not follow either rule, and it wasn't long before they were in deep financial straits. Mike and Terri closed on their first home almost to the day of their one-year anniversary. They were having a tough time making it financially even before that, but were opposed to throwing their money away on rent every month and wanted to get a house so they could start building equity. With everything they had managed to save, and everything they could manage to borrow, they bought a house for $40,000.

They already had two car loans, two student loans, and sizeable balances on their credit cards. Terri had graduated from college a year earlier and had established herself at a company where she was earning $23,000 a year. Mike was working temporary jobs while he interviewed for a full-time, permanent position. Because they managed to come up with a $5,000 down payment, Terri and Mike qualified for their home mortgage. So, without two nickels to rub together, they moved in.

They waited until their next paycheck to buy curtains; a paycheck later they bought some paint. It has been six months since they purchased their home, and today they have no furniture and Mike is working a second job to make ends meet.

As much as their determination is worthy of admiration, they probably could have saved themselves a lot of time, tears, and tension by waiting. And it probably would have put a lot less stress on their marriage. Arguing about money is one the most common pastimes for couples. But Terri and Mike don't argue about buying new patio furniture or power tools; they argue about how to pay for groceries and where they're going to come up with the money for the phone bill.

The moral of their story: think big, plan ahead, and buy small.

Use the table on the following page to calculate your monthly payment for different mortgage values. Find the current interest rate in the left column and move to the right, to the column for your mortgage term (15- or 30-year). That number is what you will pay for each $1,000 borrowed. For example, if you financed a $100,000 house at 7.5 percent for thirty years, your payment would be $699 ($6.99 x 100).

Monthly Payments per $1,000 Borrowed

Interest Rate (%)	15 Years	30 Years
7.00	8.99	6.65
7.25	9.13	6.82
7.50	9.27	6.99
7.75	9.41	7.16
8.00	9.56	7.34
8.25	9.70	7.51
8.50	9.85	7.69
8.75	9.99	7.87
9.00	10.14	8.05
9.25	10.29	8.23
9.50	10.44	8.41
9.75	10.59	8.59
10.00	10.75	8.78
10.25	10.90	8.97
10.50	11.06	9.15
10.75	11.21	9.34
11.00	11.37	9.53
11.25	11.53	9.72
11.50	11.69	9.91
11.75	11.85	10.10

Housing Options

Not everyone who owns a home lives in a small white house encircled by a white picket fence, with an apple tree with a tire swing in the backyard. When it comes to buying your first home, there are many different options.

- **Mobile homes.** For many couples, particularly those starting out, mobile homes may a plausible alternative. They're not as expensive as houses, so the monthly payments are less. Some used models cost only a few thousand dollars. When buying a mobile home there are certain things you must consider:

  1. Where will you put it? Are you going to buy a piece of property and place the trailer there? If so, you will need to budget for the

land costs and monthly taxes on that land, as well as the expense of transporting the trailer, and installing the heating, water, and electricity.

2. Does the area need to be cleared or landscaped? Does a driveway need to be poured?

3. If you're going to live in a trailer park, you will need to pay park fees, or association fees, in which case it may not make sense over the long term to park there.

One of the main deterrents to buying mobile homes is that they depreciate quickly, like cars—that is, if you buy a new one. If you buy a used mobile home and keep it in good condition, you can generally get out of it what you paid for it.

Another deterrent is size. Many people will not even consider a mobile home as an option simply because of the size. But you may be surprised. Many mobile homes have the look and feel of a rather large apartment, particularly modular units, or doublewides. Modulars and doublewides don't depreciate as rapidly as mobile homes, but they don't increase in value like conventional homes, either.

- **Condominiums.** Often called condos, these are essentially apartments you own. In addition to the mortgage payment, you will pay maintenance fees for such services as snow removal, lawn care, and other building maintenance. If you're not particularly handy or do not have a green thumb, living in a condo offers the advantage of having all of those external and internal chores taken care of for you.

  In general, the bottom has fallen out of the condo market, although some condos still sell and resell well. Because of the general perception, however, you may be able to get a terrific deal on a condo. But be prepared; selling may be difficult. Condos attract people with a certain lifestyle, and may not necessarily be the choice of a young couple who want to start a family soon. More often, they attract older, professional adults, either single or married, with no children.

- **Duplexes.** Duplexes, or doubles, can be a wonderful option, particularly if you want help with the mortgage payment, because you can live in one half of the duplex while renting out the other half. In many cases, the rent you receive will pay for most, if not all, of the mortgage. Then, if you pay off the mortgage early, that rent money becomes extra income. Another option is to rent out both halves of the duplex, and use the extra rental income to buy a new house.

Before purchasing a duplex, consider the problems of owning rental property: not finding tenants, being stuck with irresponsible tenants who do not take care of the house, lack of privacy, and being responsible for the maintenance and repair of a two-family home.

- **Town houses.** Town houses are very similar to condos in terms of the pros and cons of the investment. Like condos, there is a monthly charge for such services as lawn care, snow removal, and general upkeep. And like condos, the bottom has fallen out of the town house market in some areas, although the market value of town houses is usually higher than condos. Town houses usually have more privacy and space than condos, however. Town houses also typically have a lawn and deck area, which most condos do not. Raising a family in a town house would not be impractical at all; in fact, many families live in town houses.

  If you do consider buying a town house, get to know your neighbors on both sides. You will be sharing a wall with each of them, so it is important that your lifestyles be compatible. Better yet, get an end unit; that way, you'll only have to share one wall.

- **Co-ops.** Co-ops are very similar to condos, except that the residents own shares in a corporation that owns the building. Each co-op sets its own rules for the building, and you are a voting member. There is typically a monthly fee, called an association fee or co-op dues, for maintaining the building and grounds.

- **Traditional homes.** Far and away the most popular housing alternative for many newlyweds is the traditional home: the two- or three-bedroom house with a couple of shade trees and a nice big backyard. The main advantage of this type of home is that it will almost always increase in value, although researching property values beforehand and checking out the adjoining areas are always wise moves.

  Another advantage is that it's easier to expand or remodel a traditional home. If you need additional space at some point in the future, you can convert basements and attics into bedrooms, offices, dens, whatever, or simply add on. And finally, there is more privacy in a traditional house. You're not sharing a common wall with anyone, so you do not have to listen to their television set or vacuum cleaner. Lawn mowers and power washers on the weekends, however, are another story.

The primary disadvantage to this type of housing is that you are responsible for all maintenance and repairs: all the lawn mowing, leaf raking, snow shoveling, furnace fixing, pavement sealing, driveway tarring, shingle laying—you get the picture. And if you don't do it yourself, you'll have to pay someone else to do it. The other disadvantage, the one you'll hear most people talk about, anyway, is taxes. Single-family homes carry a large percentage of the tax burden in many communities, and the newer the community, the higher those taxes are likely to be, for such things as schools and supplemental community services.

Finding a Realtor

WHATEVER TYPE OF HOUSING you choose to purchase, you will most likely need a real estate agent, or Realtor, to help you with the transaction. Some people opt to go it alone, or hire a lawyer to look over all the paperwork, but when you're buying your first home, especially if you've had very little exposure to the industry's jargon and operating procedures, it's a good idea to have someone in your corner watching out for you.

Shop around for a Realtor the same way that you would shop around for a house. Find one who is flexible and easy to work with. Find someone who is willing to take some time with you and who has a good understanding of what you are looking for. Personal recommendations and word of mouth are often the best way to find a good Realtor.

Once you decide to work with someone, remember that your Realtor works for you. Ask for his or her advice and get explanations for things that seem unclear or confusing. Buying a home, any type of home, can be complicated. There is a lot to know and a lot of information coming at you all at once. A good Realtor will help you get through it.

Things to Check Out Before You Buy

THERE ARE MANY things to consider when buying a house. The following list of topics is not intended to be comprehensive, but it does offer a good starting point for new home buyers. As you work through the topics, don't allow yourself to become overly anxious. People regularly survive this process—they may have horror stories to tell about buying a house, but they do live through it.

Inspections

The best way to ensure you're getting a good house for the money is to have it inspected by a professional who can look at everything from basement to chimney. Many couples wait until after they have made a bid on a home to begin the inspection process, but if there are problems with the house it could greatly influence your bargaining position as well as the amount you offer. Finding severe problems could also change your mind before it's too late. Seeking professional advice is a good idea for everyone, because most couples are so busy with the "we'll put the couch over there, and I'll build my workshop in the garage" that a fair amount of objectivity is lost. When my wife and I were looking for our house, we narrowed our choice to two. But when our inspector looked the two houses over, he found structural defects in one that could have cost us plenty down the road.

Typically, inspectors charge between $150 and $350 for an inspection, depending on the value of the property. Specialized tests, such as radon, carbon dioxide, lead, and so on, cost extra. A typical inspection report will include assessments of the plumbing system, kitchen and bathrooms, heating and cooling systems, electrical system, exterior of the house, foundation, structure, yard, roof, chimneys, and crawl space or basement.

When looking for an inspector, it's best to avoid one who is recommended by the Realtor you're working with. Chances are, any professional inspector will be unbiased, but for your own peace of mind it's best to find one far removed from negotiations over the house.

Look in the Yellow Pages under "Building Inspectors" or "Real Estate Inspectors." Also, when you're walking through a house with an inspector, ask some questions, like why copper piping is so great. You're paying for his or her time, anyway, why not use it wisely? Finally, be wary of an inspector who identifies a problem and then offers his or her services as a repairman or contractor to fix it. Such an offer would represent a serious conflict of interest.

Heating

Another thing to check out thoroughly when looking for a house is heating. Whether you're talking gas or electric appliances, or gas or electric heat, the story is the same: Gas is cheaper and more efficient. In New York, for example, a kilowatt hour of electricity costs fifteen cents, compared to eight cents for the gas equivalent, for one thermal unit. What's more, gas has the advantage of so-called instant off. When you turn that knob, the gas stops. When you turn electricity off, it turns off slowly. The electric coils of your stove or heater glow a softer shade of red until they turn black, then they begin to cool. On average, gas appliances and gas heat are almost three times more efficient than electric. Below are the types of heating systems currently available and the benefits and disadvantages of each.

- **Forced air.** Forced-air heating is the most efficient heat system. A fan in your furnace blows hot air through a series of ducts to all rooms in the house. The disadvantages of forced air are (1) because air is constantly blowing through the system, the filters have to be changed regularly; and (2) hot air doesn't always make it to the room at the end of the duct. Installing an in-duct booster fan may help; for $25 or so, the fan pulls heat toward a problem area.
- **Electric.** Because it is less efficient than gas heat, electric heat should be avoided if possible. If you are looking at a home with electric heat, see if the seller is willing to pay for the gas conversion. If not, walk away.
- **Gravity feed.** Probably one of the least effective heating methods, a gravity feed furnace system looks just like a forced hot air furnace but relies on gravity to lift hot air up to the rooms above. If you've even been in a house with a gravity feed furnace during

the winter, the temperature on the main floor usually rivals the hottest day in Cuba, while the second floor approximates temperatures in Greenland. Some home owners have installed electric heat on the second floor to compensate for this temperature gap, but that's a double whammy when the bill comes. In-duct boosting fans can improve the circulation of warm air. The advantages of gravity feed derive from the fact that it doesn't have a fan blowing heat through the system; therefore, it doesn't use as much energy, blow dust around, or require a lot of filters.

- **Wood-burning stoves.** Almost twice as efficient as fireplaces, wood-burning stoves create a great deal of heat and are fairly inexpensive to operate when using coal or wood as a fuel source. The downside is the pollution they create. In fact, in some areas with a high concentration of homes that burn wood and coal, lawmakers are drafting legislation to regulate their use.

- **Pellet stoves.** Relatively new on the scene, pellet stoves look very much like wood-burning stoves, but instead of wood they burn brown pellets that look like rabbit food. Pellet stoves have the efficiency of wood-burning stoves, but without the smoke and pollution. The downside—and there is always a downside, isn't there?—is that the pellets are more expensive than wood or coal.

- **Steam heat.** Steam heat forces steam through radiators located throughout the house. They tend to be relatively efficient, plus they can add moisture to the air. People living in steam-heated homes claim they suffer fewer winter colds than people who have other forms of heat; in fact, some estimates have reported a decrease of up to one-third.

- **Oil furnace.** Much like a forced air furnace, oil furnaces force hot air through ducts, but they use heating oil to burn rather than natural gas or electricity. Oil furnaces are slightly more expensive to operate than natural gas, but considerably less expensive than electricity.

First-Time Home Buyers Programs

Many cities and counties offer special financing to first-time home buyers who qualify. Contact your city or township offices, either where you live currently or where you're planning to buy a home, to see what is available. Sometimes grants are given to cover closing costs; other times cities broker lending services and can negotiate a lower interest rate.

In addition to financial services and money-saving programs, most cities offer special classes or seminars on purchasing a home. Community education classes are typically taught by professionals in the real estate industry and cover such topics as finding a Realtor, qualifying for a mortgage, budgeting, hiring an inspector, asking the right questions, negotiating with sellers, putting in a bid, and speaking the jargon. In communities where special financing and grants are available, these classes alert students to what's out there and how to find it. It is worth the time to invest some evenings or a weekend to these types of classes. The information offered is valuable and practical, and could save you a bundle.

Visual Inventory

If the house you are purchasing is older than, say, fifty years, you'll want a detailed summary of all renovations done and when they were completed. In such a case it would be a good idea to take a contractor through the house with you to identify areas that were renovated or structurally changed since the dwelling was built. Codes change regularly, and usually for good reason.

Like any residence you're considering living in, you'll want to check out things like water (How is the water pressure? Is the water source a private well, aquifer, or surface water? Is disposal via a septic system or sewer?), lighting (Is natural sunlight available?), insulation (Does the house face east or west? Are there shade trees to keep the house cool?), carpeting and flooring (Are there worn paths? Are there scratches or scuffs in prominent areas?), walls (Are there stains? Are any nails or drywall screws poking out? Are patches visible? Is wallpaper anywhere in the house?), windows (Are they double panes? Are there storm windows? Can you feel drafts through the panes?), and so forth. But you also should dig deeper; check into health-related concerns. Take lead, for example. According to *The Family Handyman*, if the house has copper pipes and was built before 1986—that's right, as recently as the 1980s—the solder used to join pipes and fittings was probably composed of 50 percent lead. (The manufacture of lead-containing solder was not banned until 1988.) Similarly, if the house was built before the 1950s, joints between sections of water main pipe were sealed with lead, which may also be present in the drinking water. Lead could also be present in the paint. Asbestos could be in some of the insulation. Make sure your house inspector checks for these contaminants.

Be sure to pay attention to the physical attributes of the house. Look around, everywhere. Turn your head. Look up at the roof. Look closely at window frames, moldings, and soffits and fascia boards. Are they in need of paint now, or will they need to be painted within the next few years? Can you see previous scraping underneath the top coat of paint? Look down at the yard. Is the lawn well kept? Can you see mole tunnels or other rodent holes? Will you need to spend a lot of time on lawn or garden maintenance? If possible, visit the house during the day and at night. Look at the neighborhood. Is it safe? Are people hanging around on street corners nearby? How well are the streets lit?

Also remember that when negotiating with sellers, there are no hard-and-fast rules. If you like the curtains in the house, or the Persian carpet in the den, even certain light fixtures, ask the seller if he or she will throw them in with the house. Appliances are often transferred in this manner.

Glossary of Mortgage Terms

Adjustable-rate mortgage. See *variable-rate mortgage.*
Amortization. The gradual reduction of a loan over time.
Amortization schedule. The schedule that breaks down the life of the loan by each payment made, showing interest and principal paid, and remaining balance.
Balloon loan. A loan where the last payment is larger than all payments before, usually twice the normal payment, or the payment when lenders call the loan.
Closing. The process in which the ownership of a piece of property is transferred.
Closing costs. Fees and expenses incurred in the purchase of property. Costs include points, lawyers' fees, title search, escrow

payments, origination fees, Realtors' commissions, and so on. Commissions are usually paid by the seller. Closing costs do not include other costs paid at the time of closing, for example, the down payment. Typically, total closing costs average 3 to 5 percent of the mortgage value. Of course, this will vary from state to state and from lender to lender. (In some cases, particularly when the seller is anxious or desperate to sell the house, you can ask the seller to pay for part or all of the closing costs. Ask your lender or Realtor for details.)

Conventional mortgage.   Type of mortgage where buyer puts down 20 percent or more of purchase price and is responsible for all property taxes and insurance.

Debt-to-income ratio.   Ratio of monthly gross income as compared to monthly debt. This is the formula lenders use to determine how much a borrower can qualify for.

Deed.   Written document used to transfer title.

Down payment.   Partial payment needed when purchasing a home. It usually represents a percentage of the total cost, between 10 and 20 percent, but in some cases properties can be purchased with little or no down payment.

Earnest money.   Deposit put down on the property in good faith, in advance of the down payment.

Escrow.   A borrower gives a deed and/or money to an independent entity to hold until certain conditions of a contract are met. Also, lenders of FHA mortgages collect property taxes each month as part of the monthly mortgage payments and hold them in an escrow account until they are paid twice a year.

Fannie Mae.   Federal National Mortgage Association. A private corporation that assists low- and middle-income families by acquiring government-assured mortgages through the FHA.

FHA.   Federal Housing Administration. A division of the Department of Housing and Urban Development that provides financing to those who have little cash or a low income.

FHA mortgage.   Mortgage where the FHA assumes the risk to the lender for nonpayment of mortgage. Both borrower and property must meet certain requirements.

Fixed-rate mortgage.   Loan with a set rate of interest for the life of the mortgage.

FmHA. Farmers Home Administration. Federal agency that provides financing to low-income families in rural areas.

FSBO. For Sale By Owner. The owner of a property seeks a buyer without the aid of a Realtor.

Full disclosure. A requirement for real estate brokers to present all known information about a property to prospective buyers, or for a lender to disclose to borrowers the most effective cost and terms of loans.

GPM. Graduated payment mortgage. Monthly payments are less in the beginning of the loan and greater toward maturity.

Hazard insurance. Insurance that lenders require borrowers to have to protect the value of the house against such things as fires, storms, and water damage. Special flood insurance can also be purchased if the home is in a flood zone.

Homestead. State subsidy to reduce property taxes for primary residences. Homesteaded property taxes can be as much as 40 percent less than non-homesteaded property taxes.

Inspection. Examination of the interior, exterior, and surrounding property of a house to ensure quality and longevity, and that building codes have been met.

Lock in. Buyer can "lock in" at a certain interest rate before the actual closing date, usually for a term of thirty, sixty, or ninety days. Locking in can be an advantage if interest rates are rising, but if they drop, buyers must pay the higher rate.

Mortgage insurance. Insurance required by lenders, either private insurance (PMI) in the case of a conventional loan or FHA insurance in the case of an FHA loan, to protect against default. In either case, this insurance is required until the buyers have built up a 20 percent equity on the value of the loan.

Origination fee. Fee lenders charge for paperwork, staff time, and other resources used in the processing of loan applications. The fee is usually about 1 percent of mortgage value.

Owner financing. Also called land contracts, owner financing is when the seller acts as the bank. You agree on a set interest rate and pay the seller monthly payments with interest until the home is paid for. Used when a buyer would have difficulty getting a traditional mortgage. Usually requires a larger down payment.

Points. Considered prepaid interest, a point is a certain percentage of the selling price that buyers can pay the lender to reduce the interest rate on the mortgage. Each point represents 1 percent of the mortgage value and can buy down the interest rate by 0.25 percent.

Pre-approval. Approval for a certain amount of money a lender will loan. Pre-approval can help in the purchasing process, because buyers know up front how much they can borrow, and sellers are more apt to accept a bid from buyers who have been pre-approved. Many banks offer pre-approval over the phone; after answering a few questions about income and debt, buyers are given a price range they will probably be approved for (probably being the operative word here—being pre-approved does not guarantee getting approved later on).

Prepayment. Buyers have the right to prepay the principal on a mortgage, without penalty.

Principal. Amount of actual mortgage value, aside from interest. Though monthly payments remain constant over the life of a loan, amounts being applied toward interest and principal vary. See *amortization schedule*.

Purchase agreement. Written document stating buyer's intention to purchase property.

Recision notice. Notice explaining buyers' right to cancel the transaction. Federal law requires that buyers be given three days to rescind without cost to them.

Refinance. Re-purchasing the property for a lower interest rate. Origination fees and closing costs may apply, so the interest rate must be low enough that refinancing is cost effective. Home owners refinance to lower their monthly payments or shorten the life of their loan.

Rent with option to buy. Developed primarily for those who have difficulty coming up with a down payment, renting with the option to buy works like this: buyer agrees to rent property for a certain period of time, usually one year, after which time he or she has the option to buy the property and have a percentage of the rent paid go toward the purchase price. There are no set rules for these types of plans, so beware. Inspect the property before you rent, and then draw up a contract listing all terms—the percentage of rent paid that will apply toward purchase price, who will be responsible for repairs and upkeep during the rental, what is included with purchase (curtains, carpet, appliances, and so on), and who will finance the mortgage. Be sure to negotiate the best deal on a purchase price and percentage of rent going toward that purchase, and have a lawyer look over the contract before you sign.

Survey. Accurate measurement of land to determine value, borders, and area. Often required by lenders as part of mortgage process.

Title. Physical document that proves ownership of a piece of property.

Title search. Buyers can pay to have title history investigated for improper procedures, fraud, forgery, unresolved ownership, liens against property, assessments, and zone violations.

Torrens. State-sponsored system of registration for land titles. Not applicable in all states.

Variable-rate mortgage. Sometimes abbreviated VRM, variable-rate mortgages fluctuate from year to year with the federal interest rate. If interest rates go down, the mortgage interest rate goes down; if interest rates rise, the mortgage interest rate rises as well. On most VRMs, the interest rate can jump up to 1 percent per year, for five years. So if you got an ARM at 8 percent and interest rates rose every year, at the end of five years you would have a 13 percent interest rate. Also known as adjustable-rate mortgage, or ARM.

Resources

Publications

Eldred, Gary W. *The 106 Common Mistakes Home Buyers Make.* New York: John Wiley & Sons, 1994.

Glink, Ilyce R. *100 Questions Every First-Time Home Owner Should Ask.* New York: Times Books, 1994.

Irwin, Robert. *Tips & Traps When Buying a Home.* New York: McGraw-Hill, 1990.

Irwin, Robert. *The Home Inspection Troubleshooter.* Chicago: Dearborn Financial Publications, 1995.

Kiplingers Buying & Selling a Home. By the staff of Kiplingers Personal Finance Magazine. Washington D.C.: Kiplingers Books, 1993.

Miller, Peter G. *Buy Your First Home Now.* New York: Harper & Row, 1990.

Rejnis, Ruth. *You Can Buy a Home.* Stamford, Connecticut: Longmeadow Press, 1992.

Organizations

U.S. Department of Housing and Urban Development
7th and D St. SW
Washington, DC 20410-3000
For more information on FHA mortgage insurance, write for the *Guide to Single Family Home Mortgage Insurance*.

HSH Association
Dept. FTB
1200 Route 23
Butler, NJ 07405
Publishes *Affording Your First Home*, a pamphlet that contains a review of buyer fees, an amortization table, and financial worksheets.

FmHA, Single Family Housing
SW Washington, DC 20250
The Farmers Home Administration has a program of no-money-down mortgages for moderate-income families that buy in a rural area. Write for information.

The American Society of Home Inspectors (ASHI)
1735 N. Lynn St., Suite 950
Arlington, VA 22209
Write for a list of member inspectors in your area.

National Institute of Building Inspectors (NIBI)
424 Vosseller Ave.
Bound Brook, NJ 08805
Write for a list of certified business inspectors in your area.

Fannie Mae Customer Education Group
3900 Wisconsin Ave. NW
Washington, DC 20016-2899
Write for the free pamphlet, *A Guide to Home Ownership.*

❧ INVESTMENTS AND TAXES ❧

Money is like an arm or a leg—use it or lose it.
                    —Henry Ford, New York Times, November 8, 1931

Everyone—and I do mean everyone—at least once in their life
has thought about what they would do if they ever won the
lottery. In the hidden shadows of their minds or aloud in the
break room, they have daydreamed about the bills they'd pay off, the
family and friends they'd help out (yeah, right), and the things they'd
buy with $12 million or $20 million. "Twenty grand and I'm out of
debt. Then we'd buy a big house for my mom." "We'd see the world
and buy a huge Winnebago that plays 'La Cucaracha' when you hit
the horn." Or so they think.

In a recent news program, a group of lottery winners were inter-
viewed. All had won at least $10 million, but at the time of the inter-
view they were all broke. Every last one of them. Though they were
scheduled to receive annual payments for the next seventeen years,
the money was either borrowed against, or already spent. Some of
these people had even declared bankruptcy.

But before you assume a superior attitude to these people, be
forewarned: most of you will make the same mistakes with the $2
million, $4 million, or even $12 million you will earn in your lifetime. Like the lottery winners, you receive regular payments toward

your fortune and most of you borrow against it, lose it to interest payments, or have no idea what happened to it. Like those lottery winners, you have the opportunity to get out of debt, invest your money, and have more than enough left over to educate your children, travel, or retire early.

What's the trick, you ask? Investing wisely.

To many, the world of investments is frightening and alien, far too complicated for the layman to understand. "That's way over my head," you tell yourself when you hear the news that baby boomers are going to bankrupt the social security system and that you should be planning for alternative sources of retirement income. "Investing is just not meant for us common folk," you think. Well, you couldn't be more wrong. Investing is as easy as opening a checking account. And by the time you've finished reading this chapter, you will know everything you need to know to invest wisely. (Now aren't you glad you kept reading?)

Definitions

BEFORE YOU CAN discuss investing intelligently, you must first understand the terms and jargon used in the industry. Like any foreign land, you must speak the language to talk to the locals.

Stocks. A stock is an equity investment. A stock represents a piece, or a share, of a company. There are two types of stock: common and preferred. Common stock is normal ownership in a company, whereas preferred stock is stock with a claim on the company's earnings before payment can be made on common stock should the company liquidate or declare a dividend. Blue chip stocks are those with a long history (twenty-five years or more) of stable value and consistent dividend payments. Growth stocks are those that increase in share price as the company's market value increases. Basically, the value of shares goes up and down, which affects the amount of money you make or lose if you sell. (We'll forgo the explanation of market forces and economic factors that influence stock prices.) If you buy stock and sell it after its value has increased, you make money; if you buy stock and sell it when the value has dropped, you lose money. Pretty simple, huh?

Bonds. A bond is a device that allows you to loan money to someone—a business, government, utility—for a specific length of time at a determined interest rate. Just as a bank pays you interest on your savings account (and hopefully your checking account, if you are banking at the right place), the entity to which you loan money in the form of a bond pays you interest. Bond interest is paid every six months. Bonds are rated according to the issuing company's ability to repay investors. They range from safe, investment-grade bonds to risky high yields, or junk bonds.

Treasury bonds. A treasury bond is nothing more than a bond (see above) issued by the federal government and backed by the U.S. Treasury. Treasury bonds are usually held for seven years or more, and interest earned is not subject to state income tax.

Municipal bonds. Sometimes called a muni, a municipal bond is issued by a municipality, or city. Interest paid on a municipal bond is generally tax free; because of this, the interest rate is usually lower than it would be for a taxable bond. You can take your money out of munis at any time without paying a tax penalty.

Series EE bonds. Bonds issued by the U.S. government in denominations from $25 to $5,000. Interest is tax free at the state and local level, and tax deferred at the federal level unless you choose to pay the tax every year. EE bonds must be held for five years to earn the maximum rate, which goes up and down with five year Treasury note yields but cannot fall below 6 percent.

Zero coupon bonds. Government bonds that don't accumulate interest, but pay off in a single lump sum upon maturity.

Treasury bills. Also called T-bills, treasury bills cost $10,000 and mature in either ninety days, one hundred eighty days, or one year. The interest on T-bills is paid in advance and is exempt from state and local taxes. You can buy T-bills from a broker for a fee or order them by mail from a Federal Reserve bank (ask your bank for the address of the nearest federal bank or branch) without paying a fee.

Treasury notes. Treasury notes have maturities up to ten years and are sold in two- and three-year denominations for $5,000 and four- to ten-year denominations for $1,000.

Certificates of deposit. Also called CDs, certificates of deposit are interest-bearing investments offered by banks. CDs can be purchased in increments from $100 on up, with maturity ranging anywhere from a few weeks to several years. The interest rates offered on CDs vary. Usually, the longer the term, the higher the interest rate. The down side to CDs is that the investment is tied up for the entire term, or you sacrifice three months' interest on deposits committed for one year or less and six months' interest on longer-term accounts. Financial experts advise shopping around for CDs. Certain financially sound institutions can offer as much as one full percentage point above the rates offered by local banks.

Mutual funds. A mutual fund is a group of stocks, bonds, and securities that are purchased and treated as a single investment. As the value of the investments within the fund increases, the value of the mutual fund increases. Each fund's specific objectives and guidelines are detailed in the prospectus. Mutual funds are managed by professionals in the investment industry who chose each stock or bond for its potential and monitor the performance of each carefully. Investors can screen mutual funds according to any number of criteria, including friendliness to the environment, social responsibility, labor policies—or financial performance alone.

Load. Load is the fee charged on a mutual fund to pay for professional management. Loads can be as much as 5 percent, although the standard fee is between 1 and 2 percent. Some funds charge loads for buying, some funds charge loads for selling, and some funds charge loads for buying and selling. A no-load fund does not charge either.

Tax-qualified retirement plan. A tax-favored employee benefit plan that defers taxation on both contributions and earnings until withdrawn, usually at retirement age. Includes 401(k), 403(b), and Keogh (for people with self-employment income). Most companies deduct contributions from employees' paychecks (and often match them) and offer employees several choices about how and where they'd like to invest, including mutual funds, separate growth stocks, and even the company's own stock.

Annuity. A life insurer's contract providing tax-deferred earnings. Annuity income can be paid out over a lifetime or a set number of years. There are many types of annuities, but the two most common are the single premium annuity (SPA) and the deferred annuity. The SPA requires a single lump sum investment, whereas a deferred annuity requires monthly payments over a period of time. Annuities not only provide tax-deferred income, but they can serve as collateral for low interest loans. Because the loan can be paid out of the death benefit, policy owners essentially get tax-free access to their earnings. The disadvantages of an annuity are high up-front commissions, and surrender fees between 7 and 10 percent of the amount withdrawn if you cash out early in the contract. The government gets you for early withdrawal as well, charging a 10 percent penalty in addition to normal taxes on income, if you withdraw before the age of fifty-nine and a half.

IRA. A tax-deferred savings plan available to anyone with employment income. Contributions may be tax deductible (up to $2,000 a year for an individual and $4,000 for a couple), depending on your income and whether you or your spouse are covered by a pension. There is a 10 percent penalty for early withdrawal (before the age of fifty-nine and a half).

Savings/Checking accounts.   There are several types of checking and savings accounts.

- **Savings accounts.**   Passbook savings and standard savings accounts are offered by banks for people to keep their money safe and earn a nominal interest rate, currently around 2.5 percent.
- **Money market accounts.** Designed like a savings account, but interest rates are based on the U.S. Treasury auction discount rate, which is usually about 5 percent.
- **No-fee checking accounts.** Most banks, particularly credit unions, offer some sort of no-fee checking account. Charges for check processing are waived, so the only expense, if any, involved is the cost of printing checks. Often credit unions pay interest on these accounts, although the rate is low.
- **NOW accounts.** No-fee checking accounts that require a minimum daily balance, usually around $1,000. By maintaining that balance you get free checking plus interest. If your balance falls below the minimum, however, you still earn interest but pay a service charge.
- **Investment accounts.** Checking accounts that require a larger daily balance than a NOW account, usually around $2,500, but do not charge service fees. Interest is based on market conditions.

If you fall below the minimum balance, though, your interest rate drops to the level of a NOW account until your balance increases again.

Life Insurance

First, a word about life insurance. Many young people are led to believe that insurance is part of a sound investment strategy. But experts almost unanimously agree that life insurance should never be thought of as an investment: that's not what it was intended to be. Life insurance is merely a safeguard to protect a spouse in the event of the other spouse's death. It is to protect a surviving spouse from losing the house and other possessions because of the loss of income. That's it. Therefore, even though it sounds a bit harsh, you should not have life insurance on anyone who is not contributing a substantial portion of the family income. Money will not console you if your spouse dies. And in the interim, that money would be better spent in other ways.

An exception to this rule would be annuities, which are insurance policies that enable investors to put away money for retirement and defer taxes on earnings until retirement, when they will likely be in a lower tax bracket. Single premium annuities act like nondeductible IRAs in that you can put as much as you want away ($1,500 minimum) and it will grow tax free until retirement. Like an IRA, however, there are penalties for early withdrawal.

Investing: A Plan

NOW LET'S TAKE your newly acquired vocabulary and put it to work. Say you've gotten out of debt and are ready to give investing a shot. You can do that one of two ways. The first is to contact a bank or brokerage house (these are easy to find in the Yellow Pages) and see if it offers direct deposit into a mutual fund. All of the numbers discussed so far have been based on investing in mutual funds, which are fairly aggressive and usually yield a minimum return of 10 percent, although growth funds average in the high teens and low twenties.

Because mutual funds are balanced, that is, made up of high- and low-risk stocks, they are reasonably safe. Also, the people who set up and monitor these funds are experts in their field. They are brilliant at choosing which stocks and bonds will grow, and relentless when getting the best prices and options for your money. They can be a lot more effective investing millions of investor dollars collectively than you or I could be investing a few thousand dollars individually.

The second way to invest that monthly amount is to purchase these funds yourself. And the first step in doing this is, get rid of your savings account.

You'll need a place to store your money, either for emergencies or for future investment. The best "storage container" around is a money market account, which has the advantages of both savings and checking accounts and yields higher interest than both. You open it at a bank—and yes, you can still use the ATM—but instead of the 2.5 percent interest you typically earn from a savings account, a money market account averages about 5 percent. Since the money's just sitting there anyway, why not double your interest?

Many money market accounts require a minimum balance, usually between $1,000 and $2,500. You can write a small number of checks against a money market account, around five checks a quarter. And you can get a debit card, like a credit card, to withdraw money from the account. You have the right to unlimited withdrawals on a money market account provided you don't go below the minimum balance required, but if you try to use the money market account as a checking account the bank will request that you switch to a NOW account or other instrument that pays less interest. There are also money market funds which offer limited check-writing privileges (usually in amounts of $500 or more) and higher interest rates than savings accounts. Domestic money funds are invariably no-load funds.

If the minimum balance of $1,000 is beyond your reach at this point, start building up your balance in a savings account and transfer the balance to a money market account when you have enough. Get your money working for you as soon as possible, and then continue to accumulate money in the money market account. Financial planners almost universally suggest one tip in starting a savings or investment plan: pay yourself first. Write a check to your savings account or money market account as soon as you get paid. Even better, have a portion of each paycheck deposited directly. Many people think they need a large pile of cash to invest in a mutual fund, but more often than not, the initial investment is rather low—as low as $200 to start, with monthly contributions of only $50 thereafter.

Once you have more than enough money to maintain the minimum balance in your money market account, you are ready to start investing. But with so many options to choose from, where do you begin? The best advice is to start simple. Pick up a few mutual fund prospectuses and look at their long-term results. Most prospectuses will give the fund's performance over one, three, and five years, as well as for the most recent quarter. Once you decide which mutual funds to invest in, simply write one of the money market checks to your mutual fund holder each month. Eventually, you'll come to think of it as just another monthly bill, and investing will become automatic.

Once you've successfully invested in some mutual funds, you will probably feel more secure in your knowledge of the stock market and financial management in general. At that point you may want to begin looking into other types of investments, such as long-term or short-term bonds, individual blue-chip stocks, and even aggressive growth stocks. Your best bet is to find a financial advisor to plan your investment strategy and a broker you trust. After that, it's just a matter of continuing to make monthly contributions to your portfolio.

Safety First

You don't get somethin' for nothin', the saying goes. The greater the possible return on an investment, the greater the risk. Some people don't like risk, which is why there are so many safe investments such as CDs, blue-chip stocks, T-bills, and short-term bonds. But really, the best and safest way to ensure a financially secure future is by maintaining a proper balance between risk and return—a strategy referred to as "diversification."

Stocks generally deliver the greatest return on investment, but they also present the greatest risk to investors. Investors can hedge this risk, and increase the potential for long-term return, by diversifying their stock portfolio, i.e., including both safe and risky investments. In fact, according to American Express Financial Advisors, asset allocation determines more than 90 percent of the performance of an investment portfolio.

Financial experts recommend breaking your portfolio down by types of investments, and then adjusting them according to your age and financial goals. If you are younger than thirty-five, professionals recommend weighting your portfolio toward growth, which means keeping as much as 70 percent in stocks or stock mutual funds, 15 to 25 percent in fixed-income investments such as bond funds, CDs, and money market funds, and the rest in real estate or precious metals. In your late thirties and forties, you should start shifting toward more fixed-income investments. For example, 40 to 70 percent in stocks and stock mutual funds, 30 to 40 percent in taxable and tax-free bonds, CDs, and money market funds, and the rest in real estate or precious metals. By your fifties, you should be focusing almost entirely on preservation of assets. Keep some growth in the portfolio, at least 20 percent, but keep the rest in fixed-income investments like bonds and CDs, and inflation busters like real estate and precious metals.

Stock Stops

High-performance individual stocks offer the highest return of any investment you can make. But with that potential return comes risk. There is a way to reduce this risk, but it involves a fair bit of time and attention. Let's say you buy a stock at 10, meaning $10 per share. You can put a stop on the stock at 8, which means that when the stock price reaches $8 a share, a sell order is automatically processed and you sell at that price. The result: you will have only lost two points, or $2, a share. If the stock rises, on the other hand, you can raise the stop behind it. For example, when it gets to 12, you move the stop to 10, and when it gets to 14 you move the stop to 12, and so on. That way, even if it falls back to its original value, in this case 10, you'll still be able to sell it at 12 and make a profit. The down side to stops are that you lose the opportunity to ride out the fluctuations, and high-risk stocks, which are usually the top performers, are extremely volatile. An alternative way to minimize your risk when venturing into uncharted stock waters is by investing a small portion—say one-quarter—of your discretionary funds and then just see how your luck holds out.

Sometimes, though, it's best just to leave individual stock investing alone. Investing in stocks is meant for those who know what they're doing. Instead, participate in the stock market through a nice, safe, professionally managed mutual fund. Let the experts make money for you.

Investing: The Results

OK, NOW LET'S have some fun. Let's say you have decided to start investing $700 a month. What would that investment look like over time? In each of the four scenarios below, note the differences in value accumulated over the same lengths of time. Note, too, the effect of an inflation rate of 4 percent in these scenarios.

Safe

You don't want to take any real risk, but neither do you want your investment to be eaten up by inflation. So you choose the safe route and opt for bonds earning 6 percent.

Time Span	No Inflation	With Inflation
5 years	$47,352	$38,920
10 years	$110,719	$74,798
15 years	$195,518	$108,564
20 years	$308,999	$141,023
25 years	$460,862	$172,877
30 years	$664,089	$204,751

Conservative

You want to limit your risk, but, at the same time, you want to build a sizeable nest egg for retirement. You select conservative mutual funds that yield a steady 10 percent.

Time Span	No Inflation	With Inflation
5 years	$51,283	$42,151
10 years	$133,874	$90,441
15 years	$266,889	$148,194
20 years	$481,110	$219,572
25 years	$826,115	$309,890
30 years	$1,381,750	$426,019

Low Risk

You want to earn more than 10 percent, but you still want your money to remain safe. You invest in some low-risk mutual funds that yield a steady 15 percent.

Time Span	No Inflation	With Inflation
5 years	$56,636	$46,551
10 years	$170,551	$115,218
15 years	$399,675	$221,926
20 years	$860,526	$392,733
25 years	$1,787,461	$670,507
30 years	$3,651,859	$1,125,936

Moderate Risk

You decide to research some investment vehicles that offer a higher yield. You invest in some aggressive mutual funds with a small portion of your money going to blue-chip stocks. They yield an average of 20 percent each year.

Time Span	No Inflation	With Inflation
5 years	$62,509	$51,378
10 years	$218,053	$147,309
15 years	$605,095	$335,988
20 years	$1,568,179	$715,697
25 years	$3,964,641	$1,487,203
30 years	$9,927,805	$3,060,928

High Risk

You decide that the time to take a risk is now when you're young. You also have the time to carefully monitor your investment and install safeguards to control possible losses. You invest in aggressive growth mutual funds and aggressive stocks that yield a 25 percent return every year. (A 25 percent return is possible, believe me.)

Time Span	No Inflation	With Inflation
5 years	$68,939	$56,663
10 years	$279,324	$188,702
15 years	$921,369	$511,604
20 years	$2,880,735	$1,314,730
25 years	$8,860,246	$3,323,627
30 years	$27,108,264	$8,357,983

The Cost of Inflation

As you probably noticed, inflation eats up a large chunk of an investment's return. Inflation works against purchasing power, so even though your money may be growing every year, if it is earning a return lower than the annualized inflation rate you will not be able to purchase as much with that money in the future as if you spent it today. Consider these measures of inflation:

- In 1968 it cost six cents to mail a first-class, one-ounce letter. In 1996 it cost thirty-two cents, an increase of 433 percent.
- In 1969 it cost $5 to attend a Chicago Bulls game. In 1996 it cost $65, a 1200 percent increase.
- In 1966, an average Ford cost $2,000. In 1996 the cost rose to $16,000. If that rate of inflation, about 7 percent, were to continue through 2026, the cost would rise to $128,000.

Unbelievable? Maybe it seems so, at first. But in the ten-year span between 1986 and 1996, the Consumer Price Index (CPI) rose an average of 3.61 percent. Between 1976 and 1996, it rose an average of 5.5 percent. And the three years preceding 1976 the lowest jump in the CPI was 7 percent—8.8 percent in 1973, 12.2 percent in 1974, and 7 percent in 1975. That means, the thirty-year average jump in the CPI will be fairly close to 7 percent. Best start saving for that sedan now.

These figures are not meant to alarm you; rather, they are presented as argument for the urgency of planning ahead and balancing carefully the desire for safety with the need for return.

Let's say that while you were planning a long-term investment strategy, just for a kick, you asked a financial advisor to run the numbers on what would happen if you left your monthly investment of $700 in a savings account instead putting it in a stock portfolio. Here's what you saw:

Time Span	Original Investment	No Inflation	4% Inflation
5 years	$42,000	$44,153	$36,291
10 years	$84,000	$94,108	$63,576
15 years	$126,000	$150,628	$83,638
20 years	$168,000	$214,575	$97,929
25 years	$210,000	$286,925	$107,630
30 years	$252,000	$368,783	$113,702

That's right. If you left your money in a savings account earning 2.5 percent interest, in thirty years, with 4 percent inflation each year, you would *lose* money—55 percent of it—in terms of purchasing power.

In short, there is one equation that sums up the world of investing: Time + Interest Rate = Dough. The longer the time span and the higher the interest rate, the more money you make in the long run.

Investing: A Case History

HAVING SAID all this, it's time to share my own first stab at investing. If nothing else, it should at least give you the confidence to try it on your own—we all make mistakes. The first stock I bought was when my son Nicholas was born. I had $500 to stick in the bank for him, and I went and bought 163 shares of a company that was growing and had some interesting new products on the drawing board. I wasn't planning on doing anything with the money, just leaving it alone for him until college.

The stock went through the roof. I bought it at 2 3/4, or $2.75 a share, and within eight months it was at 22. My 163 shares, a $500 investment, was now worth more than $3,500, after the commission. Then, when my broker advised me to sell, I didn't. You can see where this story is going. I sold the stock about a month later for $9 a share. I still made a profit, but not nearly what I would have made if I hadn't been blinded by greed.

In addition to learning the value of listening to experts, I also learned about a thing called capital gains. Capital gains are profit made on an investment. The term has gained prominence because of the ongoing debate on Capitol Hill about the capital gains tax. One side is trying to reduce the taxes on capital gains (can you guess which side?) while the other is arguing that the rich don't need more tax breaks. Without getting too far into political ideologies, the assumption that only the rich enjoy capital gains is problematic; capital gains can accrue to anyone who invests in the market.

Anyway, back to my story. Because I kept my son's money in an account at the brokerage, I didn't think (perhaps foolishly) I would be hit with capital gains taxes. Wrong again. Every time I sold the stock, whether I left the proceeds in my account or went out and bought a satellite dish, I was being taxed.

There are a few ways to avoid this. What I should have done was open the account in my son's name, which would have been perfectly legal and ethical, since the money was for his college. I could have appointed myself trustee for the account, and everything would have been fine: no taxes until the money was withdrawn. If you don't have a child, however, you can use investment vehicles such as IRAs, 401(k)s, and Keogh plans, which enable you to defer taxes until after retirement. A word of caution about custodial accounts. Once given, usually through a Uniform Gifts to Minors Account, the money cannot be taken back. And for those fourteen and older, the first $650 of the income (i.e., interest on the investment) is tax free; the rest is taxed at the child's rate. For those under fourteen, however, the first $650 is tax free and the second $650 is taxed at a child's rate, but any income over that is taxed at the parents' rate.

Death and Taxes

AS OLD BEN FRANKLIN wrote in 1789, "In this world nothing is certain except death and taxes." It's somewhat depressing to note that these certainties haven't changed in over two hundred years.

Death

Not many newlyweds discuss death openly, but as all too many widows have discovered too late, the time to plan for the death of a spouse is sooner rather than later.

According to *Money* magazine, 70 percent of all Americans die without a will. And that percentage is greater when the deceased is young. Most young people don't think they need to draw up a will because they have nothing, or very little, to bequeath to anyone. People also believe, mistakenly, that their spouse will inherit everything automatically. But this isn't necessarily the case.

Some states have regulations set up that write a will for you when you die without one, and they rarely leave the surviving spouse with everything. Often assets held in your name alone will be split between the surviving spouse and the deceased's parents or children.

So a word of warning: draw up a will or living trust that specifies the allocation of your assets should something happen to you, and always have community property and assets listed with both spouses' names.

Taxes

No discussion on investing is complete without mentioning taxes. In fact, tax deferment and other tax-related issues have already sprung up in this chapter. Taxes are usually a dry, uninteresting topic, but they are important enough to mention here—just the basics, mind you—at least if you want to save time and frustration later.

Tax Strategies

A sound budget and investment plan should always incorporate tax strategies for the current year and well into the future. There are many strategies for avoiding or reducing taxes, and the best advice is to meet with a financial counselor or tax planner to evaluate all your options. The investment vehicles discussed so far address many of the tax implications associated with them. But what is presented here is only meant to be a starting point. These considerations will help you assess different strategies with a basic understanding of investing, but more importantly they should help you ask the right questions. There is lots to know when it comes to taxes—that's why there's an entire profession devoted to staying abreast of the information. Below are some of the areas more common to discussions of tax planning for married couples. But you will likely run into many more in your specific situation.

Pre-Tax Perks

If you've ever gotten a raise and seen your check remain almost the same or actually decrease, you know how tax brackets can affect your net income. Regardless of the particular investment vehicle you're considering, if your employer offers investment or savings plans where you have the option of using pre-tax dollars, do it. No matter what, this is a good idea because it reduces your taxable income, which determines your tax bracket. If you're on the edge of a tax bracket (say you make $100 more than the maximum income in the lower bracket), deducting your $150 IRA or 401(k) contribution before taxes will drop you down to the next bracket, which means your remaining paycheck will be taxed at a lower rate.

Tax Deferral

By taking advantage of tax-deferred investments, you can make your money grow faster in two ways. First, by postponing the tax you pay, you earn interest on the full amount of your earnings plus your regular contributions. And the more money you're earning interest on, the more interest you earn. Second, if you're like most people, you will probably be in a lower tax bracket when you withdraw the money during retirement, so you'll end up paying fewer taxes over-all—that is, assuming we don't move toward a 60 percent tax bracket sometime in the future.

Jointly or Separately?

Changing the status on your W-4 from single to married is one of the first things on the "to do" list after the wedding (see the first chapter of this book). At the time you do so, you must select either "married but filing separately" or "married and filing together." The primary difference between the two comes down to money.

Some people look at taxes as a type of savings plan and like to have more money taken out of their check so that they get more back at the end of the year. Others would rather control their own money and opt to have less withheld. If you file together (choosing the married and filing jointly option on the W-4), you will pay fewer taxes than if you file separately (the married but filing separately option on the W-4). In fact, you're almost always better off filing together than filing separately, with a few exceptions.

If one of you earns significantly more than the other—say you are in the 15 percent bracket while your wife is taxed at 28 percent—you may find that come April you'll be paying more than you would if you filed separately, because your entire household income will be taxed at the higher rate, 28 percent, and possibly even higher than that if the sum of both incomes falls into a higher tax bracket. Also, if one of you is self-employed, it may be better to keep business income and personal income separate, allowing for business deductions and keeping a safe distance should the business suffer financial difficulties.

Some couples choose to file separately just to keep peace in the house. If both partners have decided to keep their finances private, each paying certain bills every month and splitting common expenses, for example, trying to combine the finances at tax time may simply be too stressful. The easiest way to determine whether you will save money by filing jointly is to have an accountant run the numbers for you.

Choosing the Form

Short form.   Most young people file the short form, otherwise known as the 1040EZ. It takes only a few minutes to complete, and is ideal for anyone who doesn't intend to itemize deductions. Unless you are self-employed, own your own home, or have a lot of deductions, the short form is for you.

Long form.   If you own a home, are self-employed, collected unemployment benefits, or have numerous deductions, such as professional expenses, health insurance or medical costs, IRAs or investments, property taxes and mortgage interest, or other such deductions, you'll be filling out the long form this year. (Wouldn't you like to be in the governmental department in charge of naming things? "Yeah, call that one the long form ... call that one the medium form ... call that one the form with big letters and a lot of blanks ... call that one the form to request more forms.") There are two types of long forms: the 1040A is used by those who want to take the standardized deduction, and the 1040 is for those who need or want to take itemized deductions.

Filling out the 1040A is relatively simple and straightforward. In many ways, it's just a longer version of 1040EZ. Accounting software can do this type of form for you quite easily.

The 1040 requires only one step: Hiring a professional to do it for you. Unless you're really good at this type of work and have the patience of Job, it's not worth the pain and suffering you'll go through to save yourself the fee. Come to think of it, though, if you were that good at this type of work, you'd probably be an accountant. Besides, tax preparers are up on the latest tax laws and know ways to save money that you don't; in many cases, they save you enough to more than justify their fee.

Having said that, however, I should also say that it can be foolish to pay someone to file a straightforward return. The basic charge for a tax return is $50, and it can go well up into the hundreds, particularly if you have several schedules to fill out and many deductions to itemize. "But I can write off what I pay to have my taxes done," you may argue. Yes, you can, but only 2 percent of the actual cost offsets your income, so it's not all that cost efficient after all. The people who should definitely shell out the money are those involved in complicated financial arrangements, such as limited partnerships, withdrawals from retirement plans, ownership of vacation or rental property, sales of property, and investment portfolios worth more than $100,000.

Hiring a professional to do your taxes does not exempt you from record keeping, though. Don't expect to hand over a shoe box of old receipts written on cocktail napkins and a ledger that you stopped filling out in February and have the tax specialist prepare a nice tax return for you. You'll need to organize your receipts, list your spending in tax-related categories, and assemble all your information in an organized, understandable fashion. Or pay your accountant to do it for you. (Sounds like a reason to invest in an accounting software package.)

Intuit's TurboTax is probably one of the best tax software packages out there. It walks you through the long form and even allows you to file electronically. Kiplinger's Tax-Cut is a close second and allows you many of the same features. New versions come out each year and are usually available in November.

The Quick Return
Quick return companies popped up about eight years ago and have gained popularity and visibility in the last three years. These are the companies that check your tax return for accuracy and pay you your refund right away, less their 20 percent fee. They make their money on people who don't want, or can't afford, to wait four to six weeks for their return. Quick return companies resemble those check-cashing shops that take a hefty percentage for cashing a check. They charge a lot of money for doing very little, and the people who use their services tend to be those who can least afford them.

Unless you've got Vinnie "Big Guns" Dimuchi waiting at your

doorstep for his money, don't pay extra for a quick return. If you want to save some time, file electronically. Electronic filing sends your return directly to the IRS and involves no fee. It saves you time by eliminating the process of sending forms through the mail—your return is sent as soon as you hit "enter"—and by depositing your refund directly into your bank account. Think of it this way: you let the government hold your money for a year, so what's a few more weeks?

Resources

Investments
Publications
Orman, Suze. *You've Earned It, Don't Lose It.* New York: Newmarket Press, 1994.

Kobliner, Beth. *Get a Financial Life.* New York: Simon & Schuster, 1995.

Malkiel, Burton G. *A Random Walk Down Wall Street.* New York: W. W. Norton & Co., 1996.

Organizations
The Institute of Certified Financial Planners
(800) 282-7526
Call for a list of certified financial planners in your area.

Council of Better Business Bureaus
4200 Wilson Blvd.
Arlington, VA 22203
(703) 276-0100
Offers a free brochure on selecting a stockbroker. Send a self-addressed stamped envelope.

National Association of Securities Dealers (NASD)
Consumer Arbitration Center
33 Whitehall St.
New York, NY 10004

Phone (212) 858-4000
Primarily handles disputes between customers and brokers, but also distributes a number of financial publications.

Taxes
IRS Help Numbers and Addresses
(800) 829-1040 for a copy of last year's tax return.
(800) TAX-FORM (829-3676) to order extra tax forms.
Fax: (703) 487-4160
TYY/TDD: (800) 829-4059
Tele-Tax: (800) 829-4477 to listen to pre-recorded federal tax topics and check on the status of your refund.
IRS Internet Web Site: http://www.irs.ustreas.gov
Telnet: iris.irs.ustreas.gov
File Transfer Protocol: ftp.irs.ustreas.gov
Internal Revenue Information Service (IRIS), an on-line information service on FedWorld: dial (703) 321-8020 using your modem. For technical assistance accessing IRIS, call FedWorld at (703) 487-4608 during normal business hours.

Publications
Kaplan, Martin, C.P.A. *What the IRS Doesn't Want You to Know*. New York: Villard, 1994.

Lasser, J. K. *Your Income Tax 1997*. New York: Macmillan General Reference, 1996.

The Random House Book of Mortgage and Tax Savings Tables. New York: Random House, 1990.

❧ HAVING KIDS ❧

Hmyy glffth dat dat dat hii hii huu ghgkthh thh dat dat. Bye-bye.
—My son Nicholas at seventeen months,
right before he dropped my car keys down the heating duct

Shortly after our son was born, my wife decided not to go back to work but to stay home to take care of her baby. It was an easy decision for her to make, and she never regretted it.

One day I received a panicked message on my voice mail.

B-E-E-E-E-E-P

"Hey, it's me. You know that song that goes 'Nick-nack pattywack, give the dog a bone?' You know … that song—what happens when the old man plays nine? What's nine? What's nine?!?!?!?!"

B-E-E-E-E-E-P

She was frantic. Or more accurately, she had completely lost it.

There would be other messages to follow, urgent ones involving Barney and what happened on General Hospital and requests to come home at two instead of six. They symbolized how our life had changed forever.

For many young couples, having children and raising a family is a given. You get married and buy a house, and then you have children. It's the natural order of things. It seems so natural, in fact, that many couples want to start a family fairly quickly after getting married. Sometimes too quickly.

Key West

MY WIFE AND I wanted to start a family right away. But when we got married, money was a little tight. Later on, it was just as tight: with both of our incomes pooled together, we had enough to pay our bills, put some macaroni and cheese on the table, and maybe splurge for a an occasional movie or dinner. We had taken a short honeymoon, three days in the Poconos. But besides that, and occasional weekend camping trips, we had never been on a true vacation together.

One night, on the spur of the moment, we decided to splurge and go away together. We decided to take a week off and go on an official plane-flying, over-the-state-line-traveling, hotel-staying, luggage-checking-in vacation! Key West, Florida.

If you've never been to Key West, I suggest you quit your job, sell everything, and go right now! It's like no other place in the world.

Without recounting the fun, laughs, romance, and adventure of our trip, suffice it to say we had the time of our lives. A month after we returned, we found out that Debbie was pregnant. In some ways, the pregnancy was the perfect conclusion to a wonderful trip. It was also the conclusion to a life of just us two together.

Every couple needs to find their own Key West. This type of time together is important in a couple's life. It allows you to bond to one another. Not like the bond you formed while you were dating, or planning your wedding, or buying a home, but a deeper, closer bond. It is a time when you can get to know your mate as your mate.

If you are like most couples who stay together, you will probably look back on your first few years of marriage fondly. Finding two nickels to rub together may be tough, the apartment may be small, but remembering those nights of dancing together in your living room to the music of the neighbors' party upstairs, or those silly paper and popcorn chains you will hang around the windows as holiday decorations, will conjure up a special feeling. Despite the new cars you will have in the garage twenty years from now, or the five-bedroom, professionally decorated house, or even those $700 suits in your closet, these early years will be the most special. They lay the foundation for your future, as a couple and as parents. This is your time together as adults in love, not parents-to-be, not parents, not grandparents.

While there is no formula or checklist to complete to see whether or not you are ready to have children, there is one thing you should remember: It is impossible, physically and emotionally, to give anyone else more than you have yourself. That means, if you are a disappointed, unfulfilled person, you cannot "get it together" to give your child unselfish, supportive love. If you are unhappy or filled with regret, those emotions will be passed along to your child. You must have your own life and be happy within it to pass along the sense of completeness, fulfillment, confidence, and happiness your child must learn from you.

Now, that doesn't mean you must reach all your goals before you start your family. The process of working toward them is what's most important. Knowing you are striving for something, growing emotionally or spiritually, learning intellectually—these are the activities from which you build strength and fulfillment. Basically, you cannot be the parent—or the spouse, for that matter—you want to be unless you are becoming the you you want to be.

Aside from that, there is no hard-and-fast rule for when you should start a family. Some experts recommend five years. Others say three. But really the best time to start your family is whenever you feel you are ready to. End of point. But there are some factors to at least consider.

Money

If not abundant, your finances must at least be flexible, because once you start your family everything will change. There will be diapers, bottles, teething rings, and formula to buy, and wee sizes of everything: toilets, walkers, tennis shoes, snow pants, towels. If nothing else, the "that's so cute" reflex takes over your wallet. All of a sudden, it seems reasonable to spend $25 or even $50 for less than a half yard of material and a little lace trim.

According to *Parenting* magazine, depending on a family's income, the average cost to raise a child from birth to the age of three is between $7,000 and $10,000 a year. That includes housing and transportation, and other costs you are already paying for, as well as food, health care, and other costs that will increase with the arrival of

Junior. Costs go up slightly within certain age increments, until the child reaches fifteen, when the cost runs from $9,000 to $12,000 a year until the child reaches seventeen. The costs of raising children eighteen and older is much more variable. It's not unheard of today for young adults to live at home until they are in their early twenties. And parents who can afford it often help support their children right through college, including paying for tuition, books, room and board, and for the lucky few, even a monthly spending allowance.

But back to the beginning. One of the first things to consider when thinking about having a child is the size of your savings account. Do you have some money put away for those extra things you will need? All a baby really needs, of course, is love, physical care, and more love, but there are definitely some things that go a long way toward making parents' lives easier. Among them: a baby seat if you're planning to take your infant anywhere in the car; a changing table if you want to stand upright after two years of changing diapers; diapers, again, if you're planning to take your child anywhere that letting him or her run around naked is inappropriate; a stroller if you're not planning to enroll in the Olympics weight-lifting division; the list goes on and on. Then there are the clothes, formula, bottles, pacifiers, blankets, and cute little toys you simply cannot pass up.

Many of these items can be handed down by relatives or given as gifts at baby showers. But there are other ways you can save money, too. For instance, shop garage sales, particularly in the spring, when many baby items are sold—some of them hardly used. Second-hand shops, too, sell "gently used" baby items and clothing for a fraction of the cost of brand new. It's nice to have new baby things, but keep your impulse to buy in check. If you're financially unprepared for parenthood, it's wise to save money wherever you can. There will be plenty of expenses later on, believe me. Between sports equipment, school field trips, "in" fashions, and inflation-adjusted allowances, you'll be digging for spare change in the couch cushions for some time to come.

Another financial consideration is health insurance. If you currently have insurance—and I sincerely hope you do if you're having a baby—assess the adequacy of coverage: What is the deductible? How much will you pay out of pocket for the delivery and hospital stay? Are well-baby visits covered? If you're planning on starting a family soon, it may not be a good idea to change jobs. Many health insurance plans classify pregnancy as a pre-existing condition and require that you be employed for a specified number of months before providing pregnancy benefits.

While important, financial considerations should not constitute the sole criteria for determining when you are ready to have a child. As my Aunt Ida used to say, if you wait until you can afford a child, you will never have one. It's important to plan ahead and be prepared for parenthood, but there is a time to step back and accept that human beings have been having kids for four thousand years. Some things just have a way of working themselves out.

The Inevitable Changes

THE BEST WAY to describe what it's like to be a parent is, you no longer think of yourself—and you like it. There's no other experience that can compare with it.

Children are a gift from heaven. The love you feel for your child is like no other on the planet. Experiencing that special love is only one of the many gifts of having children, though. My son Nicholas has given me many other gifts as well: a broken nose, a slice of individually wrapped cheese inserted into my disk drive, 1,261 lost hours of REM sleep, an extra twenty-five pounds, and a bulky pair of eye glasses brilliantly redesigned to a more convenient, two-piece set.

There's also the fear that becoming a parent will turn you into your own parents. The image of me wearing black socks with sandals and talking to the thermostat haunts me at night: "What, am I paying to heat the outdoors?"

Then there's rivalry. Not the sibling rivalry you engaged in as a child to eke whatever extra attention you could from your parents. No, this is adult rivalry, a competition between friends about such trivial matters as drool, sitting up, and blurting out unintelligible sounds.

"Tara has been sitting up for weeks and is crawling now."

"Oh, Trevor decided to bypass the crawling stage and go right to walking."

"I guess Tara has been too busy talking to concentrate on

developing her motor skills."

It gets ugly, believe me. And don't think you won't do it. The impulse is beyond your control. Something inside you jumps and twists in a knot at the possibility that another child can do something yours cannot. This internal jumping bean lasts at least until adolescence, when you'd sooner remove your right thumb than compare the accomplishments of your teenager with that of another, or even share stories of his or her exploits.

There is one definite perk to having a child—did I say one? I meant millions—you get to be a total idiot in public places. You suddenly have an excuse to walk around the grocery store making gurgling, cooing, hiccuping noises at your toddler in the grocery cart. What's more, people just smile and think you're a wonderful parent.

And remember that dinner party angst you felt? No more. You will no longer have to worry about people being bored. Family and friends will be entertained for hours, just by watching your child perform his repertoire: "What does a doggy say?" "What does a kitty say?" "What does a cow say?" "What does a pig say?" "Now let's do 'I'm a Little Teapot' for Uncle Glen and Aunt Carrie." For friends who don't have kids, however, watch the repetition. More than likely, twenty choruses of the Barney song will more than suffice.

But those are all the fun perks. There's also an emotional and spiritual maturity that comes from having kids. At the risk of getting too philosophical here, it comes from a sense of connectedness.

The Connection

REPRODUCING, PERPETUATING the species, has, for many, a profound effect on the way they see and experience the world. All of a sudden, the future becomes more important. That favorite phrase of so many politicians, "what we are leaving our kids," takes on a whole new meaning. For "our kids" means your kids. No longer are the world and its inhabitants separate. Instead, the world is a place your kids will explore, learn from, influence, and affect.

It may sound corny, but it's true. Even if the bottom drops out of my day, when I come home and see my son's smiling face as he runs to the door, everything falls into perspective. Suddenly, nothing is as complicated or infuriating as I thought it was an hour before. The world is reduced to Sesame Street action figures and bubble baths, first steps and first tumbles, smiles and gurgles and sloppy kisses, and by the time I get my coat off and loosen my tie I've forgotten what it was that got me so stressed out in the first place. And I get to be two years old again.

"This old man, he plays nine. He plays nick-nack on my spine."

A TWO-BLOCK HEADSTART

Here's a story
of a lovely lady
who was bringing up three very lovely girls …
                    —*Theme song from* The Brady Bunch

In middle-class America there is a standard scenario for moving from youth into adulthood: boy and girl go to college, boy and girl begin their careers, boy and girl meet, boy and girl marry, boy and girl buy a house and start a family. What's standard for some, however, is necessarily standard for all. For example, not every student goes on to college right after high school: some don't go at all, some go after they've been in the work force for a while, and some go in their thirties and forties. Likewise, not all adults have successful careers when they meet their spouses. Some—indeed, many in today's climate—are still struggling. And some start their families with one spouse and then get divorced or are widowed, and so they already have children when marriage rolls around a second time.

Any time two families merge, any time a single parent marries, or two divorced parents get married, a new combined family results—an insta-family, a unique hybrid. Nowadays, few families fit neatly into the classic American family mold: two parents, two children, one dog, and a goldfish. At least, I know of few that do.

The Insta-Family

IF YOU HAVE married someone with children, you're finding that you must learn to adapt to those children as well as to your new spouse. And if you both have children, you could have any number of people trying to adapt to one another all at the same time. In such an environment there's bound to be some disruption, if not outright chaos.

Attempting to make sense of the dynamics of insta-families requires a master's degree in psychology at times. Unlike Mr. and Mrs. Brady, you may not have the help of an Alice to keep things sane and to help solve little squabbles. And problems probably won't resolve themselves within a thirty-minute time frame the way they do on television. However, there are some basic guidelines that you can use to help your new family cope with change.

1. The children come first. If you're marrying someone with children, you're getting a package deal. You must decide beforehand whether or not you are ready for that commitment and whether or not you can commit to your spouse's children in the same way you are committing to your spouse.

2. Involve the children. It's important to make children feel a part of the new family by involving them in everything from the decision about getting married to the actual ceremony.

3. Be open. Discuss feelings openly with everyone present. Show that everyone's voice and feelings are important to you and to the entire family. That means allowing children to say what they feel, even if you don't like it.

4. Show both groups of children you care. The family is one unit, even if it is made up of your kids and your spouse's kids. Now, they're all yours, and you must treat them so.

5. Treat each child the same. This doesn't mean talk to them about the same topics or make sure you issue the same number of bologna slices to each child; rather, it means to expect everyone to follow the same rules and to treat one another with respect. There should be natural consequences for breaking rules; punishments should not be negotiable.

6. Give them time. Don't expect that you will be one big, well-adjusted, happy family by Sunday. Give everyone time to adjust to their new life. After all, you and your spouse made the decision to get married, not them.

7. Be a friend first. Don't rush in with new rules and tough love. Kids often feel threatened by a new spouse, particularly when a parent has died. When the surviving parent gets married, children feel they will lose the attention and love of the only natural parent they have left. They need reassurance, so don't get caught up on titles or respect now. Maintain the house rules, certainly, but be a friend first.

8. Set aside alone time to spend with your natural children. As important as it is to conduct yourself as a new family, it's also important to allow children to retain old family relationships. If you take that away, they may see their new environment as not only a change, but a loss.

9. Don't force it. Kids, like all people, bond at their own pace, and if you try to force certain feelings on them, they will rebel.

10. Be patient. Everything may seem overwhelming, especially at first, but it's not. Kids respond to love and unity. They respond to feeling included, a member of something bigger than they are. You've just made a new family. You've created a group out of strangers, and while the road ahead will be bumpy, everything will work out eventually.

There are some basic questions that arise when families are blended. They include the following:

- **What if the kids don't like each other?** This possibility frightens many newly married parents, especially with teen-aged kids who can be quite vocal, if not downright hostile, toward one another. Believe it not, though, many natural siblings go through a similar stage. If you treat each child as an important member of the family, the "I wish I didn't even know you!" squabbles will be minimized.

   Try to find interests step-siblings share in common, and family activities everyone will enjoy. Whether it's sports or movies or a hobby, get the kids involved together. Sooner or later, family memories will be created, and the kids won't be so concerned about whether or not they are biologically related.

- **What if the kids don't like the new spouse?** As noted in rule

7 above, kids naturally feel resentment toward a stepparent, especially if he or she is trying to discipline the child. "You're not my father (or mother)" is the single most common response when kids think a stepparent is trying to take the place of their natural parent. The response is an attempt to establish some autonomy and self-responsibility. It is also the first thing that comes to mind when they're being told to do something they don't want to.

Instead of feeling defensive and arguing about your right of authority over them, listen and hear what they are telling you: They don't want you to act like their parent just yet. Even though it may sound like rejection, it's actually a hint about the role they'd like you to take, that of a friend or mentor or just someone else in their lives who cares about them. Sit down with each stepchild and come up with a plan together. Make it clear that you don't intend to take the place of their mother or father, but you do want to be involved in their lives. (This is where rule 5 comes in handy. If all the kids have to follow the same rules, no one can accuse you of trying to control their lives.) See if you can find some common ground where you can both get to know one another. Offer to help them with homework or work on improving their curve ball—whatever you can do to help them. You will soon earn their respect, and they will know you can be counted on.

- **What if a stepchild tries to play one parent against the other?** Children will use flattery, criticism, complaints, lies, exaggerations—whatever they can think of—to divide and conquer. They think they will get away with things by pitting one parent against another. And they will if you play along.

  The first thing to do when your child complains to you about your new spouse is listen. Even if the actual events they recount are false, the feelings are still important. Second, talk to your spouse. What your child is telling you may or may not be accurate or real, but be careful not to put yourself in the position of believing one over the other. When stories don't agree, it's best to sit down—all three of you—and hash it out until you get to some common ground. To do this, it's best to focus more on feelings than actual events.

  While children often play one parent against the other, the

behavior is particularly significant in blended families. First of all, it lets you know that your child is feeling threatened, for whatever reason. Second, it's a chance to sit down and talk, really talk, with your child. Third, your child may be pointing out a real problem in your spouse's behavior. Remember, your children are part of you. They should be made to feel that what they think and how they feel matter, to you and to your new spouse. Take the time to deal with the problem.

Natural Parents Getting Married

MANY COUPLES live together before getting married, and some of these couples have children before they marry. In these cases, the parents may have been raising their children for so many years that they feel no need to talk about parental relationships, child rearing, and so on. However, it may be important to explain what is happening anyway. It may be confusing to children that their parents are getting married all of sudden. What does it mean? How is it different from before? How will it affect the family?

When Death Is Involved

WHEN A PARENT dies, a child may develop an idealized image of that parent. Cuddling by the fire, joking around and laughing, going out for an ice cream in the summer—the good memories are played over and over again in the child's minds. Bad memories, on the other hand, tend to be shoved to the back of the closet, out of respect for the deceased.

The death of a parent can be difficult to deal with in a new marriage, because you're not only trying to overcome the child's natural resentment at your being in his or her parent's life, you're also trying to live up to a saintly ghost. "My mother never would have done that! She was much better than you." "If my father were still alive, he wouldn't let you do this to me! He loved me!" You are being told not only that what you are doing at the moment is unacceptable, but also that the child is feeling sad or missing his or her parent. These are the feelings to focus on.

Try to get children to talk about their feelings, or share a memory they have of the parent. Allow them to experience their grief, but keep it separate from what is going on in the present. Be gentle, and be respectful, but do not compete with a ghost. It's a battle you'll always lose.

Two Families: Two Sets of Rules

WHEN CHILDREN GROW up with divorced parents, they often have two sets of rules: one for Dad's house and another for Mom's. This same principle can be carried into a new marriage. New family, new rules. Set up house rules at the beginning. And if they differ from previous rules, that's OK. The point is to establish them and maintain them. Do not be swayed by what the other parent reportedly does at his or her home. In fact, what you are hearing may not even be close to what is actually going on in the other parent's home. You and your new spouse must set up rules and expectations you both can live with, involving children in the process as much as possible (see rule 2 above).

A final note: if your house has numerous rules, allow time for adjusting, within reason. Maybe everyone gets one freebie or one legitimate "I forgot"; but after that, consequences kick in. Setting up the introductory phase could be part of the family discussion about new rules and new consequences. Get your children's input about what they think is fair. And if they are having a hard time adjusting, consider reducing the number of rules. Some experts recommend having ten rules that cover everything. That way, everyone knows them, and you're not having to rack your brain to remember the rule, clause, and subsection that deals with curfews during the school year.

WORK, CAREER

Commuter—one who spends his life
In riding to and from his wife;
A man who shaves and takes a train,
And then rides back to shave again.
                    —*E. B. White,* The Commuter

I remember my father once saying something so profound that I actually listened. Sitting in his flannel shirt, he said, "In my day, you wore work clothes to work and dressed up to go out. Now you wear suits to work and jeans to dinner."

Just as I was about to compliment him on his insight, he began to tell the story of riding the train from Albany to Tokyo, which went right into what we affectionately referred to as the railroad medley—a collection of twenty-seven of my father's favorite stories, all blended together into one long tale. I had heard them enough that I could have recited them by rote.

Times have changed. The one-income homes of the forties and fifties are now few and far between. People have a completely different set of directions and goals for their career. The more ambitious and driven people are, the more they are envied and respected. In the past, things like family, church, and community were more important than careers. In the past, people worked to live; now people live to work.

In the early sixties, the average family income for a newly married couple was $5,000. The income for a doctor or other experienced professional was between $15,000 and $20,000. Today, the average income for a young couple starting out, with both partners working, is around $30,000 a year. A seasoned doctor will gross somewhere between $200,000 and $300,000 a year. Look at the difference between the two incomes, for both time periods. In the sixties, the ratio of high wage to low wage was three to one. Now it is more than twice that: seven or more to one. The wage gap has widened substantially.

That's bad, or good, depending upon who you ask: Surely, those who are in the seven-or-above category aren't complaining. On the other hand, those in the second half of that ratio—the "to one" category—probably would have liked it better in the sixties. "Liked earning $5,000 better than earning $30,000? Surely, you jest," echo the objections, most likely from people in the seven-or-higher category. But the $30,000 only looks better if you don't figure in inflation. Though people today make a great deal more money than their parents or grandparents did, that money is worth less in "real," inflation-adjusted dollars.

People today need to work smarter and harder than their parents and grandparents did. They need to do more with less, get more done in less time, achieve more with fewer people. Layoffs and downsizing, global competition, job insecurity—these are the standards of corporate life today.

What has all this to do with the first year of marriage? Nothing, directly, but indirectly, career and the pressures of career can greatly affect a marriage, particularly in the first year. Work and careers play a bigger role in people's lives than they did just a few years ago. Careers now require more time, more energy, and more attention than they did in the past. Because the demands of a full-time career can be all-consuming, many people are having to seek whatever intellectual, social, and emotional fulfillment they can find, in their jobs.

Identity

IN THIS AGE of the sound bite, people want to be able to sum you up in thirty seconds or less. People need to know what type of box to put other people in. Are you a factory worker or a test pilot? Do you teach chemistry at Columbia or sweep floors at Jefferson Senior High? Just consider what happens when people meet you for the first time, for example. What's the very first thing they ask? "So, what do you do?"

People's careers give them a sense of identity. All too often, unfortunately, their entire identity. While defining yourself entirely by your job can be unhealthy for anyone, it can be particularly toxic in a marriage. Marriage is a partnership. As a partner, you must create a couple identity, a united image that incorporates your partner. Otherwise, the marriage is just a convergence of two separate individuals, plodding down the same path at the same time. But at any time that path may twist or turn, or an alternate path may become available. When such changes occur, only a couple identity will keep the union intact.

One effective way to build and maintain your identity as a couple is to set some goals together. Just as you must plan your future with regard to such things as budgeting for a house, investing for retirement, and setting up rules for children, your individual life goals should be discussed and shared. There are three types of goals people usually set: professional goals, self-improvement goals, and personal goals.

Professional goals involve work and career, obviously, but they should involve more than that. Professional goals should reflect your desire to do something special with your life, to help others as much as yourself.

Self-improvement goals are more individualistic. Maybe you always wanted to learn a foreign language, or wished you were better at meeting people. Maybe you'd like to lose weight or get in better shape. Everyone has something they would like to change about themselves, and support from a spouse can help them make it happen.

Personal goals are related to both professional and self-improvement goals. They run the gamut from taking ten points off your golf game to running the Boston Marathon some day. They may be as simple as reading a book or as involved as writing a novel. The point of a personal goal is that you do it for yourself.

As a couple, sit down and share your goals. Tell each other where you'd like to be in five or ten or twenty years, how you'd like to feel, and what you'd like to be doing. Let your partner know the real you.

And then make a commitment to each other and to yourself that you will strive for your goals and will help your mate strive for his or hers.

An additional note about setting and achieving goals: It isn't necessary that you achieve all your goals. What makes people happy is knowing they are working toward something they want. It's the process rather than the end result that matters most. And dreams change over time, anyway. Even if you've never realized your dream of becoming a professional hockey player, you can still actively participate in the sport. Be a coach, open a hockey store, start a hockey newsletter, play hockey with your friends, develop a hockey fan Web page. Keep your dreams alive by allowing them to grow and evolve as you do.

Support

IN A MARRIAGE, one partner's success is the other partners' success as well. It is crucial to understand and acknowledge this, so both partners can not only share in the joy and excitement of the accomplishment, but also get due recognition for their effort and contribution.

The key is to support each other—in everything, whether it's career or developing the perfect fly-fishing technique. One of the perks of marriage is having someone to share the good times with.

Stress

ALL TOO OFTEN, particularly in today's corporate climate, the price of success is stress. And not just the normal stress that comes with day-to-day living. Today's stress can be overwhelming.

People handle stress differently. While some are able to leave their stress at work, many more take their stress home with them. Some people never talk about stress, while others let it out in any number of ways, verbally, physically, and emotionally.

However you handle it, at some point in your marriage, stress will affect your relationship. Stress builds up in your body—it burns in your gut, it affects your mind, it even creeps into your dreams. Thus, whether you talk about it or not, it's part of your marriage.

Stress Relievers

There are both positive and negative ways to relieve stress. Driving down to the El Camino Tap to toss back eight or nine cold ones relaxes you for a time, but the next morning you still have the problem and, worse, now you're throwing up neon and can't find your car. Likewise, if you're stressed out about money, shopping until you drop is probably not the best course of action.

Far and away, the most effective method of getting rid of emotional and intellectual stress is physical exercise. It doesn't matter whether you climb a mountain or clean out your garage, just do something physical. Chemicals produced in the brain during exercise, called endorphins, help to relieve stress. In fact, people who exercise regularly can achieve a quasi-meditative state during exercise—a state characterized by clarity of thought and peace of mind. In addition, the cardiovascular benefits of getting the body moving can help to reduce, if not eliminate, the physical manifestations of stress, including gastric problems, depression, heart disease, hypertension, sleep problems, and exhaustion.

Of course, you won't even know that you need relief unless you're sensitive to the signs of stress. This means paying attention to your body's warning signs: increased heartbeat, heightened agitation, rage, headache, fatigue, physical aches (especially in the head, neck, and shoulders), nausea, even dizziness.

Monitoring your own stress level isn't enough, however. As a married person it is also your responsibility to monitor your spouse's stress level. (I'll bet no one mentioned that before the wedding, right?) This gets easier with time. After a few years of seeing your mate's moods, reactions, and stress levels change from day to day, you'll soon learn to recognize his or her physical symptoms of stress and you'll know when to prescribe jogging, a hot bath, or other stress busters.

My wife takes mini vacations. Once a month or so, I'll sneak home early on a Friday, and we'll have a quick dinner. Then she'll leave. Her mother is gone on weekends, so she'll head over to that big quiet house for the night to spend a relaxing twenty-four hours at a place where "The wheels on the bus go 'round and 'round," is not played. Barney is not welcome; it's just her, alone with a book, a nice cup of tea, and whatever relaxing music she cares to listen to. The arrangement works well for me, too, because it gives me some alone time with Nick so I can teach him how to skip rocks, burp on cue, and do other important things that his mother neglects to teach him during the day.

Pinpointing the Source

"What causes your stress?"

Many people would answer that question without hesitation: "It's my boss; he's so demanding." "That project started it all; once it is finished, my life will be much calmer." "That client just expects the moon; there's no way we can deliver." Usually, however, the source of the problem is closer to home.

Most people feel stress as a reaction to feeling powerless and overwhelmed. Often that feeling is simply due to a lack of organization or time management. A project seems too big, out of control; you feel like you're just spinning your wheels, getting no results. In such cases, it isn't so much the problem itself that's stressing you out, it's your inability—or refusal—to define and delimit that problem.

Lack of Time

One of the primary causes of stress is having too much to do and too little time to do it. Making a list can help to relieve this sort of stress. Actually, it's not just making the list, it's systematically eliminating items on that list that can instill a sense of accomplishment and relieve stress.

The key to using lists is prioritizing. First, write down all the things you need to get done. Begin with the big picture; you can break down projects into individual tasks later. Look at your list and identify the single most important item on it. Ask yourself, "If I can only get one thing done today, what should it be?" Circle that item. Be demanding with yourself, but don't decide that everything on your list must be done by noon or your world will end. That type of thinking is only self-defeating.

Once you pinpoint your top priority for the day, focus solely on completing that task. By concentrating and working exclusively on one single item, you will be able to work more efficiently, and you just may surprise yourself by getting it done faster than you thought you could. Once that task is completed, cross it off and repeat the process, answering the question this time, "If I can only get one more thing done today, what should it be?"

Time is a rare commodity for many newly married couples. Those newlyweds who both have demanding and stressful jobs may see precious little of each other during the week. In fact, I know of many couples who consult their DayTimers just to schedule an occasional lunch or weekend away. If this is the way it was before you got married, you are most likely used to it by now. But if it's the result of a career or title change, it may be difficult for you, especially if you're accustomed to having alone time together. Suddenly your wife is traveling more or your husband is working more nights.

The good news about time is, it can be managed. Tricks of time management will be discussed in more detail in the next chapter, but for now, just remember this: you may not have time to do everything, but you will have time to do the important things.

Problem Solving

Worry is a great contributor to stress. In fact, worrying about a problem can be more stress-producing than the problem itself. It can even exacerbate the problem by causing a person to avoid or procrastinate about dealing with the problem directly.

Therefore, the most important step in solving any problem is acceptance. First, define the problem. Then, identify the worst possible thing that could happen as a result of this problem. Are you going to forfeit your promotion? Lose some money? Be arrested? Be honest with yourself. Bouncing a check will not mean that you'll have to declare bankruptcy, so don't punish yourself by fantasizing that it will.

Once you've identified the worst possible result, accept that you will be able to live with it should it happen. Simply accepting that you can go on if something bad should happen will probably make you feel better. And once you've brought the problem out into the light of day, you can go to work to prevent the worst-case scenario from happening.

At the top of a sheet of paper, write your problem in the form of a question. For example, "How can I get $400 by the end of the month?" "How can I find a better job that pays more money?" "How can I reduce stress at work?" Now list twenty possible answers to your question. Don't limit your responses. Let your thoughts go. You're asking your mind to solve a problem; you can't give it a task and then limit the results. Banish the critic. List all solutions to the problem as if it were a riddle. Even if it looks like the second or fifth answer is the solution, don't stop; keep going until you get twenty.

When you are done, look at your list. Choose the best possible solution and try it. By identifying something you can do about a problem, you've transferred the energy you spent worrying about it into actually doing something about it. This shift alone will leave you with a sense of relief, as will solving the problem.

Balance

"YOU CAN HAVE it all," women's magazines proclaimed in the seventies and eighties as they profiled superwomen in power suits who managed to enjoy successful careers in the day time, while keeping house, cooking meals, and raising children at night. Huh? How'd she do that? The good news is, child-rearing and household duties are no longer considered the sole responsibility of the female. Now, it's up to both partners to divvy up the chores, so to speak, and to share equally in the mundane and time-consuming tasks required to live in this society. But can both partners have it all?

Sure, they can, but not with a picture-perfect life. More realistically, partners who both work, pursue extracurricular hobbies, stay fit, make time for each other, go on outings with friends, and keep up with all the housework and grocery shopping do a delicate balancing act. If you visit them during the week, you will probably see magazines and newspapers laying around their living room, dirty dishes or pans in the kitchen sink, piles of laundry heaped in front of the washing machine, the iron and ironing board still set up in the bedroom, and the backyard doggie area in need of some cleanup.

But does that count as balance? Yes. In this day and age, balance means putting certain things off, particularly unimportant things like doing the laundry or keeping a spotless kitchen, to make time for more important stuff—things that can't be put off without losing your health, your job, or your friends: exercising, socializing, spending time together, keeping up with the job, and so on.

Part of this balancing act involves keeping work and career in perspective, and that means involving your spouse in your career without letting your career dominate the relationship. Your mate can be a valuable resource for your professional development. Even if unfamiliar with your particular job or business, he or she can be an excellent source of honest feedback. Many professionals use their spouses to bounce ideas off, or role play asking for a raise, or discuss possible solutions to a problem. You spend more of your waking life at work than anywhere else. Doesn't it make sense that you would want to hear how your spouse spends his or her time at work?

On the other hand, you don't want your career to become the only thing you share with your spouse. Set some guidelines for your time together. If, for example, you're going on a weekend getaway, discuss your work days and problems on the drive Friday night, but then focus on each other and on other more personal issues for the rest of the weekend. Many couples can go overboard in sharing stories about work and career, so it's important to have other interests and discuss other topics with each other. After all, you didn't marry your spouse's job; you married the person.

❧ TIME ❧

A wonderful stream is the River Time,
    As it runs through the realm of Tears,
With a faultless rhythm, and a musical rhyme,
    And a broader sweep, and a surge sublime,
As it blends with the Ocean of Years.
                                    —B. F. Taylor, The Long Ago

Next to a short line at the Department of Motor Vehicles, time is one of the rarest commodities around. Particularly in the first year of marriage, it's important to pay attention to time, not only how much time you need, but also what type of time you need, and how your partner's needs differ from yours.

Alone Time

SOME PEOPLE need lots of alone time. Some don't need any. Some want to spend every waking moment with their spouse; others need some one-on-one time with close friends as well. Alone time is somewhat misunderstood, particularly by those individuals who don't require a great deal of it. Alone time means just that: time spent by yourself, alone. Alone time is time to relax or do the things you like to do alone, such as running or biking or reading or taking a drive or going to a movie, whatever.

Sometimes, people who don't feel the need to spend time alone interpret a request for alone time from their partner as a rejection. Because they don't need time away from their partner, they don't understand why their partner needs time away from them. Hurt feelings and even distrust can result.

"She would rather be alone than with me?"

"He would rather be with his friends than with me?"

"She would rather be working than with me?"

But alone time is not about someone else; it's about you. True, if you're spending time alone, you're not with another person, but alone time is the need to spend time with yourself, not to be away from someone else.

Couple Time

COUPLE TIME is time spent with each other. It can be the two of you alone, with another couple, or with a large group of people. However, most people do not consider time spent with others as quality couple time.

As with alone time, it's important to know how much couple time you need and how much your spouse needs. If you're a person who requires a great deal of couple time, you may find it difficult to understand why your spouse needs alone time or time with friends. You may view your spouse as selfish or uncaring, and your spouse may see you as clingy or stifling.

Work Time

AS DISCUSSED in the preceding chapter, work time is taking up more and more of people's lives. The forty-hour work week is a rarity; more likely, a typical work week ranges between forty-five and fifty hours a week. When working to meet a deadline, that total can surpass sixty hours a week, which leaves little time for anything besides work. And in addition to the actual time spent in the office (unless you are one of the lucky ones who works at home), there is also what I call "cognitive" work time. That's the time you spend thinking about work, calling the office, planning your day, recounting the stress of the day to your mate, and so on. When you factor in this additional time, the enormity of work's influence on people's time—for that matter, on their lives—becomes apparent.

Because the previous chapter was dedicated to work and career, I won't discuss work time any further here, except to point out that most couples consider it untouchable, nonnegotiable. After all, they must work to live.

Friends Time

FRIENDS TIME is important to many, particularly people with long-standing, close friendships. These people have spent years cultivating their relationships with friends, and their attachments do not dissolve when the marriage certificate is signed. As with alone time, however, people who have little need for friends time find it difficult to understand their partner's need for it. They often see friends time as time lost, and the friends as being in direct competition with them.

What Type of Time Do You Need?

PEOPLE'S NEEDS for time have very little to do with their relationship as a couple and almost everything to do with their individual personalities. It's important for you and your spouse to know the type of time each of you needs as well as the quantity of that time. Look at those times in your life when you feel stressed, when you feel happy, when you feel frustrated. Are you alone? With your partner? With friends? Now compare your inclinations with those of your spouse? Are there some obvious conflicts? What do you do when your time needs conflict significantly with those of your spouse?

In the Central Time Zone

THERE ARE SEVERAL ways to resolve differences between your time needs and those of your spouse—to find your own Central Standard Time. For example, you can schedule your time alone in advance. That way, the time will be set aside before you need it, which will help avoid negotiation under stress. Conflicts are much more likely to arise when people impose their needs on other people unconditionally and without notice.

The key is to be consistent, but flexible. Your mate who needs a lot of couple time won't mind if he knows that every Wednesday night, for example, you'll be unavailable. If plans change, however—and they always have a way of changing at the last minute—it is important to allow your spouse some flexibility. If your mate calls after a stressful day at work and says she is going to cool off for a while and will be home late, you must give her the space she needs to recover.

Respect and communication are just as important. If you do need to change the schedule—say, a buddy calls and offers you tickets to the playoffs—call and negotiate an alternative with your spouse. If you suggest a sort of trade, chances are that your spouse will be receptive, as long as no formal plans have been made, of course. Think of couple time as a formal date and treat it accordingly. Just as you would not have broken a date when you were courting without arranging another time in advance, you should not do it now. Or, at the very least, be aware that such behavior may land you in the doghouse.

A Time Imbalance

Time conflicts arise in a marriage when a person who needs a certain type of time, say alone time or friends time, marries someone who doesn't. More than likely, a conflict is simply a lack of understanding. People have a difficult time empathizing with you if you don't communicate your needs. If you have married someone who has different time needs than you do, try to explain your needs. If you need some alone time, explain to your mate why you want to be alone: to meditate, to think, to daydream, to read, to write, to relax. Your partner is likely to be more understanding if you tell him or her what you're going to be doing with your alone time rather than act secretive or aloof about it. Certainly, you have the right to set aside some time for yourself. But you also have the responsibility to help your spouse understand the benefits you derive from being alone.

Don't simply give in to your partner's insecurity, though. Denying your needs puts stress on the relationship. You may start to feel stifled or caged in, and you will resent the feeling—and your partner for making you feel that way. Stand your ground, but be respectful about it. Help your spouse get to know you and your needs. It will only help you fulfill them in the long run.

Recycling Time

EVEN AFTER you've identified the type of time, and how much of it, you need, there's still the question of where you can find it. After all, everyone knows there's never enough time. Right?

Well, that may seem true in most cases, but it's all a matter of how you look at it. There does seem to be enough time for most adults to watch between four and six hours of television a day, for example. And there is always enough time to go out with the gang for a night on the town. And then there are those informal gatherings after work that stretch out until 8:00 at night. The point is, no matter how busy your schedule, there's enough time to do the important things. What you have to learn to do is "recycle" your time.

Recycling time involves two components: finding time and prioritizing time. Let's begin with finding time. At the end of any given weekday—after work, dinner, cleanup, and miscellaneous chores—there are probably two to three hours left before you usually go to bed. That's between ten and fifteen hours during the work week that can be recycled and used for couple time, alone, or time with family and friends.

Just as you had to learn how to budget your money, you must learn how to budget your time. And the first step is seeing where your time is going. Take an average week, one that doesn't have unusual obligations such as a niece's recital, heavy work deadline, or holiday party. Go out and buy another one of those thirty-nine-cent pocket notebooks that you used to write down everything you were spending (be sure to account for this notebook in your budget).

Start on Sunday morning. From the time you get up, jot down everything you do. Divide each sheet into two columns. In the left column, keep track of the amount of time you spend doing things—for example, how long you read the newspaper or talk on the phone. Track everything for a week, resisting the urge to judge how you're using your time. You're just gathering raw data, not correcting your time-spending habits.

After a week, add up all the time spent. If both of you kept your own notebooks, total your time. This will enable you to get a good look at how you spend your time as a couple as well as how you spend it individually. (It will also tell you whether you are perceiving couple time the same as your spouse.) On a separate sheet of paper, list your activities according to how much time you spent doing each. Write the activity you spent the most time on first and work your way down to the activity you spent the least time doing.

Now look at your list. How many hours did you spend watching TV? On the phone? Doing laundry? Commuting? You may be surprised by how much time you spend doing certain things. This is the step where you find time. Just as you were able to find extra money you were spending on nonsensical things, you can pinpoint time you're wasting. First, see if there are some activities you can combine. For instance, can you fold the laundry while you watch TV or while you talk on the phone? Can you spend time alone reading while you're at the Laundromat? By combining some of your activities, especially busy work with down time, you'll probably be able to eke out an extra few hours each week.

Next, write a list of how much time you would have liked to have spent on each activity. This list should reflect your priorities. For example, if you would like to spend more of your time reading than watching TV, this list should reflect that.

Now, compare your lists. How much time did you actually spend reading? Was it more or less than what you would have liked? How much time did you actually spend with friends? Was it more or less than you would have liked?

In these discrepancies lie recycling opportunities. Go through your lists with your spouse, discussing activities and times that can be overlapped and consolidated. Combine activities that you once did separately so that you can spend more couple time together. Bike riding, for example, or even grocery shopping, could become couple-time activities, whereas reading or working out could satisfy your need for alone time.

I'm a person who needs a great deal of alone time. When my wife and I were first married, we set up a weekend schedule. Saturday mornings I'd get up early and write for an hour. Then around 6:00 I'd wake Debbie up by taking some fresh coffee in to her, being the wonderful, loving, attentive husband that I am.

Debbie worked Saturday mornings, so as soon as she left for

work, I'd leave behind her. As she would be pulling out of the driveway in her car, I'd be flying down it on my mountain bike. I'd head for my office for a few hours and get some things done while it was quiet and then ride over to the health club. After working out, I'd ride back to the house, and if I timed it right I'd be out of the shower by the time Debbie got home. Then, we'd have the weekend to use however we saw fit. I'd get five good hours of alone time, and then we'd spend the rest of the weekend doing couple things—all on recycled time.

Resources

Bliss, Edwin C. *Getting Things Done*. New York: Bantam Books, 1976.

Josephs, Ray. *How to Gain an Extra Hour Every Day*. New York: Dutton/Signet, 1992.

Rechtschaffen, Stephan, M.D. *Time Shifting*. New York: Doubleday, 1996.

𝕰 FIGHTS 𝕰

I love the smell of napalm in the morning.
—*Robert Duvall,* Apocalypse Now

If you've noticed a recurring theme in this book, you're right. The theme is, the importance of communication. It's an old theme, but a good one. The preceding chapters have offered strategies for improving communication. What this chapter deals with are the consequences of not communicating.

Generally speaking, a couple will fight more in the first year of marriage than in the next three, or even five, combined. It's true. In a recent poll of newlyweds, 37 percent said they were more critical of their mate after they were married. Add to that the mixture of change, adaptation, and stress that accompanies the first year of marriage, and you can see why fighting is practically the main pastime in the first year.

Well, not exactly. But it is common. Couples fight during the first year of marriage for many reasons:

1. They're letting their hair down, so to speak; they begin to be themselves.
2. They're discovering, or voicing, what is truly important to them.
3. Their expectations are not being met.
4. They see change as a loss and resist it.
5. They feel restricted.

Types of Married Fights

JUST AS THERE are numerous reasons for fighting, so are there many types of fights in marriage. A married fight is often several fights combined into one: It's a roommate fight, a sibling fight, a best friend fight, a coworker fight, a business partner fight. Because your spouse is all of those people in one, if just one of them does something that angers you, you lash out at the whole person.

Communication Fights

The communication fight is not only the most common type of fight between newlyweds, it is the most common type of fight between any two people. The communication fight is, as the name suggests, caused by poor communication. A communication fight results when couples send messages that are unclear, when they misinterpret messages, or when they fail to send messages at all.

Communication fights can result when one spouse fails to call home, leaves a curt message on the answering machine, or makes plans without consulting the other. Say, for example, that you go out with fellow office workers after work and end up staying later than you had planned, but you don't call your husband. When you get home, a few hours after he expected you, your husband greets you with, "Where have you been? Why didn't you call?" After explaining that Teresa was having a crisis and you didn't feel you could leave, he is still angry, mumbling under his breath as he stomps out of the room, "You didn't even care enough to make a phone call."

A couple of things are happening here. For one, you have yet to take responsibility or apologize for your lack of consideration. For another, your husband does not feel that his concerns have been acknowledged; he assumes that your lack of consideration means that you don't care about him. The result: you end up fighting about something that could have been avoided with better communication.

Treatment

An adage has sprung from communication fights: "If you're still talking, that's half the battle." Talking it out, keeping the lines of communication open—that is the key to resolving communication fights.

It is when spouses stop talking to each other that small rifts fester into deep wounds. These rifts will heal only if you continue to express your feelings to each other. Share your feelings, your secrets, your desires, your pain. By sharing you not only let your partner know you, you learn about yourself. And sometimes, although not always, as soon as your words hit the air you realize how silly your reaction or assumption was, and your interpretation changes.

One helpful tool for keeping communication open is to focus more on the effect of an action than its cause. For example, instead of saying, "You roll your eyes at everything I say!" try rephrasing it with your own feelings: "I feel humiliated when I see you roll your eyes at something I've said." Or, instead of "You were so busy that you couldn't even find two minutes to pick up the phone and call me? I was sitting here waiting for you!" try talking about how your spouse's actions made you feel: "I was so worried when you didn't come home, and I feel disrespected that you didn't think to call me."

Focusing on the effect rather than the cause softens the sense that you're attacking your mate. Your spouse hears a reasoned point of view rather than angry accusations that elicit defensive feelings.

Expectations Fights

More often than not, our expectations exceed reality. In fact, about the only time things turn out better than imagined is when we aren't expecting much in the first place.

When my wife and I were first married, we'd occasionally take short day trips. We'd have no special route for the day; we'd just see where the road took us. My wife was rarely disappointed on these trips because she only expected to go to a nice restaurant, or a lake, or a winery. I, on the other hand, had much less realistic expectations.

I imagined that an exciting, life-changing adventure fit for a Paramount Pictures script would surely unfold. Maybe we would pick up a hitchhiker on the run from the mob and help him escape, or maybe I would be wrongly accused of a robbery and Debbie and I would have to go on the lam. Or, maybe Debbie would get kidnapped by terrorists and I would have to use my Navy Seal training to save her. Anything like that would have been fine. But what usually happened was, we'd drive around for a while, I'd get lost, we'd get something to eat, and then we'd try to find our way home.

I tried to sell that script idea to Paramount, but they wouldn't return my calls.

Expectations can be a trap. When an activity or event meets your expectations, the experience often seems flat: it was adequate; you expected as much. And when an activity or event does not meet your expectations, it's a disappointment. So rarely does an activity or event exceed our expectations, it's no wonder that young couples sometimes feel a letdown in the first year of marriage. The odds are, marriage is not always going to be as great as you expected it to be.

Treatment

The human mind has the capacity to create a picture that would give even the best Super Panavision a run for its money, complete with Dolby sound and 3-D imagery. So when people finally sit down to watch the black-and-white movie projector that is reality, with no sound but the humming of the motor, of course they're disappointed.

The best way to avoid being disappointed is to discuss your expectations with your spouse. If you have a clear picture in your mind of how you want something to be, tell your partner. As you articulate what you've imagined, you may see that part or all of it is unrealistic, in which case you'll be able to change your mental picture without feeling short-changed. If your expectations are not unrealistic, telling your partner is the best way to make it happen.

Where couples get into trouble is by quietly attaching very specific expectations to certain "big" events: a romantic Valentine's Day, a cuddly Christmas Eve in front of the fire, a private New Year's Eve celebration. Some women daydream romance into their relationships and celebrations, only to be disappointed when their husbands and boyfriends don't deliver. What they fail to incorporate into these fantasies is who their chosen men are—for example, expecting a man who watches football every weekend to make plans for a romantic weekend getaway in November. Expectations that fly in the face of who your mate is and how he or she lives life are sure to fall flat.

During this first year of your marriage, take the time before special events, celebrations, holidays, and other occasions, to talk about your expectations. Share your own mental image of the event and listen to your partner's. Then talk about each set of expectations. Do some of them appeal to both of you? Are they compatible? Could you make the upcoming date fit your picture? Don't underestimate the power of spontaneity, though. Sometimes, the best traditions and the most heartfelt memories begin with life's little surprises.

Lifestyle Fights

When people who are comfortable with single life marry, they are sometimes reluctant to give up their old habits and ways of living. Lifestyle fights are often the result. One spouse is holding onto his or her lifestyle, wanting the other spouse to squeeze in without disturbing anything. This does not necessarily mean that the spouse doesn't want to get married, or is uncaring. Rather, it's more a power struggle to keep a lifestyle that is familiar and comfortable.

Treatment

Lifestyle fights will accomplish one of two things: Either two styles will slowly merge into a single comfortable one, or resentment and hurt feelings will build up as one or both partners resist change. Share your mental image of your lifestyle, and listen to your partner share his or hers. How do you want to live your life? How are you living it now? How does your spouse fit in? How do you see your lifestyle changing in the future? The name of the game in resolving lifestyle disputes is, communicate, communicate, and then communicate some more. Oh, and be fair.

Values Fights

When people think and feel differently about moral or ethical issues, a values fight may occur. This type of fight is usually characterized by one spouse feeling that something the other has done, or has thought, is wrong. The reaction is largely an emotional one. One spouse is not only bothered by what the other is saying, but the way he or she sees the other becomes distorted. All of a sudden, the person that spouse has cared for, looked up to, and been in partnership with is not the same.

Usually values disputes are over small things. Most likely, your wife will not come home tomorrow reporting that she's decided to knock off a liquor store. She may say, however, that the sales clerk gave her $5 too much in change and she kept it. Some people would consider this luck; others would see it as stealing.

Treatment

If you're lucky, you will already have worked through many values issues while you were dating. Most couples get to know one another's basic values in everyday conversation and by noticing how the other reacts to certain situations. If nothing else, they discover these things while they're planning the wedding. In the case of a short engagement, however, or an unusually smooth planning process, values differences may not appear until after the marriage.

Again, if you're lucky, differences in values will fade over time, as you grow and evolve together. If they don't, you could be in for many years of fighting. Then your choice is either to keep things to yourself or pay the price for sharing it—a price that will usually involve one of those day-long, heated discussions at the kitchen table. Of course, if there are extreme differences in values, you will either have to agree to peacefully coexist or else go your separate ways.

Spiritual Fights

Like values, spiritual issues can provoke fights between newlyweds. Spiritual issues go beyond ethics and morality, beyond mere right and wrong. They often manifest themselves more as feelings than ideas, and a spiritual disagreement is more of a sense of discomfort than a fight. Although spiritual fights may involve religious principles or traditions, they are not necessarily about religion. Spiritual differences occur more frequently in marriages where there are significant cultural differences—in interfaith and interracial marriages, and in marriages where spouses have different ethnicities or countries of origin.

Treatment

Everyone has a spiritual side. The difference is, some people are more aware of it than others. Discussing spiritual issues may be difficult for those people without well-defined convictions on the subject—difficult, but probably not impossible. Again, if you're lucky, spiritual issues will have surfaced before you got married. If not, and one arises, approach the topic gently and respectfully. Spirituality often involves deeply held beliefs, and denying or arguing a spouse's beliefs can cause permanent wounds. Even if you and your spouse do not feel the same way about a particular subject, at least by discussing it you will both realize what is important to you.

Goals Fights

Ah, the future. That one common ground you have as newlyweds, regardless of personality, religion, ethnicity, gender, profession, or blood type. When you became engaged, you implicitly agreed to work together toward a common future. And during the wedding ceremony, you explicitly vowed to stay together until you're old and gray. Hopefully, you still feel that way.

If you're like most people today, you probably have goals you're working toward. If you're young, you may be working to buy a house with a picket fence, two cars, and two-point-five children. Or you may want to finish college and move to Paris to be an artist. Your goal could be to get your career off the ground before starting your family. If you've already started your family, your goal may be to send your children to college. If you're a member of the post-baby boom generation, one of your goals is probably to save enough money for retirement. Whatever your goal, part of marriage is working toward it together.

Goals fights occur when one spouse feels resentful of the other's lack of support or encouragement, or disagrees with the other's direction. For example, imagine coming home one night to hear your husband exclaim that he's just quit his job and is going to stay home and become a writer. He tells you he's thought his plan out: six months will be plenty of time to become famous, so until then the two of you can cut corners and live off of your salary.

Besides the fact that your partner may be in some physical danger from you right now, there are obviously a few things wrong with this picture. First, your husband has made a major life decision without discussing it with you, a decision that will affect both of you and may cause great financial difficulty. Major decisions should be made jointly, and after careful consideration. Second, new goals, especially major goals, take time to adjust to. Not that you shouldn't stand by and support your spouse's convictions and plans. But when those plans differ dramatically from past behavior and goals, some adjustment time is necessary.

Even worse, the goal in this case is a selfish and unrealistic one. Your husband has done something irrational—namely, quit his job—for an idea that, as far as you know, he didn't have when he left for work in the morning. And he has given himself a ridiculously inadequate time period for succeeding in a competitive field in which he has no experience.

Compare that to another scenario. Your wife comes home and excitedly reports that she wants to try writing as a part-time job. She is eager to break into the field because she feels she's been putting it off for too long. This scenario makes much better sense than the previous one. First, the wife has shared with her husband something she is excited about and wants to try. Second, her plan of attack—wanting to write part-time at first—shows that she is patient and willing to take the steps necessary to succeed as a writer.

Treatment

The key to resolving goals fights is to be considerate. Even if your spouse wants to fly to the moon, remember that by telling you about a goal, your spouse is sharing something important to him or her. Consider the feelings involved. The more important the goal, the stronger the feelings. And being rational doesn't always come with the territory. If your spouse is excited about something, you should try to be sympathetic to those feelings, even if you think the plan leaves something to be desired.

Everyone wants to be supported and feel accepted. If your wife is excited about a goal, she wants you to be excited about it, too. If your husband is disappointed about a setback, he wants you to share that disappointment. Without reciprocation, a spouse can feel rejected, and become angry. Make sure you give your spouse the same sort of encouragement you would want from him or her.

Now, that doesn't mean you have to sell the furniture and begin sewing your space suit. If your spouse is way out there, reel him or her back in. But do it gently. Even if goals are unrealistic, they still were borne of dreams and imagination, which are part of your spouse's soul. Often, a gentle reminder or a few thoughtful questions can help get your spouse back on track. What's more, by engaging in a practical discussion, you'll be showing your spouse that you believe in him or her and that you're taking his or her goals seriously.

No-Fight Fights

Only one person is talking, but two people are fighting. When one spouse argues with the other who just sits there contributing nothing, you have a no-fight fight. Ever heard the phrase, "It's like talking to a wall"? Most often, people who don't fight—actually, people who don't argue—learned at a young age that fighting was wrong. In fact, in most cases, these individuals learned that talking loudly was wrong. "Fighting is bad, so I won't fight" is their plan, and they avoid it at all costs. But the fight goes on, even though only one person is participating verbally.

Of course, arguing with someone who won't even talk gets frustrating. Paradoxically, the passivity and silence of one partner can escalate the intensity and volume of a discussion, which can cause the non-fighter to withdraw even further: "Must avoid ... Danger ... Danger ... Danger ... Shut down all systems." Most likely, the non-fighter is simply reacting to the emotion and volume and doesn't even hear what is being said.

Treatment

Non-fighters cannot be trained to fight. It goes against every fiber of their being. They can, however, be talked to calmly. The best bet when dealing with non-fighters is to keep the intensity level low. If the subject of the argument is simply too volatile, however, the spouse who feels the need to scream should try to get it out of his or her system in another way—say, screaming at a pillow or engaging in a physical activity to work out some of the aggression—and then try discussing the matter later, when feeling a little calmer.

Stress Fights

When you live with a person day in and day out, you see them at all times of the day: in the morning, after work, before bed, during sleep. It is illogical to assume that you won't be together at a time when one or both of you are feeling stressed. And it is even more illogical to assume that you'll never get on each other's nerves or snap at each other, regardless of how wonderful you both are.

Particularly in your first year of marriage, when things are still new, and change is so rapid and frequent, tensions and stress will cause a fair number of squabbles.

Treatment

Accepting that fights will be part of your marriage is the key to keeping stress fights in check. They are going to occur, no matter what. So don't sweat it when they do. Give each other some space, without assuming that it means the doom of your marriage. A temporary spat here and there simply means that you're both thinking and breathing human beings.

As you get to know each other better and get used to living with one another, you will come to realize that the two of you simply communicate differently. It is not necessary to check out how your spouse reacts to every look, every statement, every question, every glance. When you were a child and would yell or snap at your brother and sister, you wouldn't go running after them every time to see if you hurt their feelings. Same thing here.

Gender Fights

At the risk of reinforcing gender stereotypes, I think it's safe to say that men and women tend to exhibit different modes of behavior and patterns of communication. Or at least experts say such gender-related traits are common. According to Ladies' Home Journal, for example, men tend to see complaints as an attack, and blame their wives for upsetting them. Men tend to jump into a problem with a quick fix rather than to just listen, which is often all that women want. Men also tend to shut down when their wives become emotional. Women are more likely to speak with a blaming tone of voice, complain about what their husbands don't do (without acknowledging what they do do), and try to change their husbands by offering unsolicited advice.

Treatment

According to the *Ladies' Home Journal*, the first step toward dealing with gender fights is to make a list of the topics you fight about most. Then, get a timer and a tape recorder. Set the timer for twenty minutes and record a conversation about one of the topics on your list. By listening to the tape, you'll be able to hear yourself: tone of voice, patterns of blaming or accusing, habits of interrupting. Then, you can identify the patterns you want to change and be mindful of them when communicating with your mate.

Letting the Sun Go Down

YOU'VE PROBABLY heard the phrase "Let not the sun go down upon your wrath." Or maybe your Aunt Elsie just pulled you aside at your wedding and told you, "Never go to bed angry, dear." The idea is the same in either case, and originates from the same source: a bestseller called the Bible. Actually, almost every book ever written on marriage has something to say on this theme.

But is it good advice? At the risk of sounding blasphemous—can a Christian disagree with the Bible?—there are exceptions to this rule. In my own marriage, my wife is the person who cannot go to sleep until we settle a fight. She thinks I am uncaring if I fall asleep before we resolve all our disagreements. But my reaction in situations like this is to shut down. "Let's go to bed and talk about it tomorrow," I say.

Morning has a certain magic to it. It makes things new. It provides a new beginning every day, and for me, it is emotionally calming. In the morning, I feel refreshed, more able to make sense of what is being said and more likely to see the errors in my thinking. I am able to focus my attention on the content of what is being said instead of on the tone of voice and language being used.

But letting something wait until morning only works if both partners are able to sleep, which means that the fight cannot be too significant. In general, if one or both partners are too upset to get a good night's sleep, it's worth staying up to hash it out. Otherwise, I say, night, night.

The "I'm Sorry" Rule

FOR MANY PEOPLE, once a fight is over everything is simply forgotten and the world is a wonderful place again. Others require that an official declaration of remorse be declared and conditions of forgiveness agreed upon. Which brings us to the "I'm sorry" rule. Some individuals use I'm sorry's sparingly, and, as a result, seem more sincere when they do extend an apology. Others dish them out like Halloween candy:

Mud on the floor? I'm sorry.

Forgot to get milk? I'm sorry.

The Dow Jones fell today? I'm sorry.

Whether you should apologize depends upon how your spouse feels, so it's important to know where you and your spouse stand on proper "I'm sorry" etiquette.

The same thing with forgiveness: some require a verbal confirmation ("Apology accepted" or "That's OK"), while others prefer actions, such as a hug or a kiss, and some require no response at all. What is important is to know what you need and what your spouse needs, and to act accordingly.

❧ PHYSICAL FITNESS ❦

At least you have your health.
—My Aunt Ida, at any particular time

It's ironic how much people seem to care about their physical possessions and how little they seem to care about their physical selves. They clean and polish their cars, for example, tune them up, and change the oil every 3,000 miles—they do everything they can to keep their cars in shape for the five to ten years they own them, yet they neglect their own bodies, which they will have for the rest of their lives. People's bodies are their personal vehicles. Women carry their children in them; men bounce their grandchildren on them; they get us around for seventy, eighty, even ninety or more years.

People who are in shape generally catch fewer colds, remember things better, think more clearly, and sleep more easily. On average, people who are in shape make more money, are more successful, and are generally happier than those who are not. People who are in shape look better and have more energy. Oh, they also live longer. But while these are plenty of reasons to stay in shape, the true motivation for most people who take care of their bodies is an emotional one: they feel better about themselves when they are confident about their appearance. Which is also a good reason for newlyweds to stay fit, because how spouses feel about themselves affects the way they feel about each other.

Unfortunately, many people have skewed notions of what it means to be fit. They think that being in shape means that you can crush a beer can with one hand, or that you have to look like you just stepped off the cover of an aerobics video. But being "buff" doesn't necessarily mean you're fit, just as being thin doesn't necessarily mean you're healthy and being fat doesn't necessarily mean you're out of shape. Fitness is a balance of three things: flexibility, cardiovascular endurance, and muscle tone. Period.

Ever see someone who lost a great deal of weight by simply cutting back on fat or watching what they eat? They look better, certainly, and they're probably healthier nutritionally, but are they in shape? What about that skinny person you know at work who eats jelly donuts for breakfast and cheeseburgers for lunch, and doesn't exercise, yet never gains a pound? Or what about the guy who does nothing but exercise on his StairMaster day after day?

In some remote piece of my memory, I have stored the notion of something called the golden mean. The phrase comes from Horace, who in 65 BC wrote in his book *Satires*, "Whoever cultivates the golden mean avoids both the poverty of a hovel and the envy of a palace." Modern day translation: Nothing to excess. All things in moderation. That guy on the StairMaster may be in great cardiovascular shape, but he probably lacks muscle tone and flexibility. Likewise, that skinny person may have the genes to stay thin, but he's not likely to be physically fit at all.

In this fitness-conscious age, fat is a hot topic. People are programmed to think they have to get rid of all their body fat to be healthy and attractive. Attractive, maybe—it depends who you ask—but healthy, absolutely not. I'll say it again: being thin has very little to do with being in shape. A person in shape may have a lower ratio of body fat to muscle than someone who's not in shape, but being thin or muscular is more the result of fitness than its cause.

The No-Time to Work Out Workout

THE MAIN OBJECTION most people, particularly newlyweds, have to getting and staying in shape is that they don't have enough time.

"There are no health clubs around me, and I work such long hours…." "I travel a lot, and it gets hard to fit it in…." Schedules change during the first year of marriage. Stopping off at the gym for an hour or so on the way home from work may have been fine in your single days, but now there are dinner plans waiting on you or a spouse in dire need of some love and attention.

My wife and I met in a health club. I was her aerobic instructor. True story, so stop laughing. I was working as a buyer of electronic equipment for a subcontractor firm during the day, and teaching aerobics at night and on weekends. My wife saw me, her heart started racing, and her entire life changed as she began an obsession with making me her own. Or something like that, anyway.

We started dating, I changed jobs, and we eventually got married. In the beginning, I worked out three times a week, played tennis one night a week, and rode my mountain bike whenever I got the chance.

Then came Nicholas.

A lot of stuff happened before that, but with the arrival of Nicholas things really changed. I accepted a better job, which brought with it more responsibilities, longer hours, and considerably more rich, fattening meals with clients. You can see where this is going. It was no longer as easy to exercise. I was working weird hours, Debbie needed help with the baby, and if I had had a long day and had to choose between working out or being at home with my wife and son, I'd choose to stay home.

Every Monday without fail, I'd try to get back into the habit of exercising. Once in a while, I'd actually fit in three workouts in the same week, but then the next week only two, then one. It wasn't long before my clothes didn't fit right, I got winded going up stairs, and I was always tired. Finally, I got on a scale: I had put on twenty pounds.

When I recovered from the shock, I remembered a quote I had once heard: the definition of insanity is doing the same thing over and over and expecting different results. Now, I wouldn't say I was ready for a white suit and a rubber room, but I was dangerously close. My attempts to establish an exercise routine weren't working, yet I continued to try the same thing again and again, convinced that each time it would work.

I had to find a way to get back into shape, a new method that would really work for me. So I went to the Thirty-Nine Cent Notebook Store on Fifth and Broswell and bought myself one of their famous thirty-nine-cent notebooks. It was blue. I started writing down my frustrations. I knew what to do, but I couldn't find an hour three times a week to do it in. What I could find was ten, fifteen, even twenty minutes here and there. So I came up with a system.

I weighed myself and took some measurements that are too humiliating to record here. Then, I made a grid of the first week, dividing a piece of paper lengthwise into seven rows and three columns. The rows were for the days of the week, and the columns were for the three exercise elements I knew I needed: flexibility; muscle toning and strengthening; and cardiovascular endurance. The idea was that I was going to get in three, twenty-minute routines in each of these boxes, every week.

The first day I managed to get some stretching in. The second day I actually got to the health club to get a quick twenty minutes on the Stairmaster. I was planning to do some more that night, but the lawn had to be mowed and I had to run back to the office and.... So, the third day I completed a quick toning routine during my lunch hour. Though I only got a few minutes here and there, the effects started to add up. My system was working. Sometimes I was only getting half a routine in, but I was feeling better and people were noticing the results. I kept track of my progress in my little notebook, and by the end of the week, my ten minutes here and ten minutes there had turned into three complete cross-training workouts.

In four weeks I had jump-started my energy level, my mind was sharper and quicker, I felt more organized and in control, I could take more than two steps at a time without wheezing, and I had lost six pounds and an inch of fat.

If time is not an issue, an ideal fitness plan would involve a cardiovascular and muscle-toning workout three times a week, plus a fun physical activity or game that you could enjoy one or two nights a week. In half an hour to forty-five minutes at a health club, you can get a twenty-minute cardiovascular workout and squeeze in a quick toning routine. Then play tennis, go for a walk, take up a martial art, join a volleyball team, go canoeing—do any physical activity you enjoy or always wanted to try.

Body Memory

HOW MANY PEOPLE have you known who have gone on strict diets, lost a few pounds, then put all that weight back on and more? It's called yo-yo dieting, and eventually, when people complete the cycle a few times, the weight loss process stops working entirely. Pretty soon, they cannot even take off the initial few pounds. The human body has a memory. It goes something like this: "OK, we've been through this drill before. Just hold tight and we'll be back on schedule in a few weeks."

The same thing happens with exercise. After a time, your body becomes accustomed to your schedule and sends out a message to level off. And you plateau. Whatever return you're striving for—weight loss, muscle mass, muscle definition, lung capacity, muscle strength—diminishes over time. Thus, it's important to trick your body, sort of. A good way to do that is to change your routine every four to six weeks, especially the toning or muscle-building regimens.

Health Clubs or Home Workouts

IF YOU HAVE a schedule that allows you time to get to a health club three times a week, take advantage of it. In the great debate of health clubs versus working out at home, health clubs will win every time. At a health club, there are trained staff available who can help set up a safe and effective program and answer questions along the way. In addition, it's easier for most people to stay motivated at a gym or health club because visions of fitness are all around.

There is also the benefit of location. Because most people incorporate going to a club on their way home from work, a schedule develops and the thought process becomes automatic: "If I stop by right after work, I'll get my workout in and still have the rest of the night." At home, however, there is always time to do it later. If you don't feel like exercising now, you can put it off until after dinner, or after you straighten up, or maybe you'll get up early and work out before work....

Of course, depending on your current level of fitness, there may be an intimidation factor at the thought of going to a health club.

Most people who are overweight or out of shape would rather not put themselves on display. After all, they'll never measure up to the "beautiful people." But not all health clubs are like that; in fact, few of them are. There are only so many beautiful people, and if you live anywhere in the country besides Manhattan, New York, or Hollywood, California, your chances of finding a gym that only serves actors and models are pretty slim.

Before you talk yourself out of getting your body in shape because you have misconceptions about the atmosphere at a gym, go for a visit. Take a tour. Drop by to take a gander, without your workout clothes. Most likely, you'll see people like yourself trying to improve their lives one muscle at a time. If you don't particularly like the first club you visit, go to another. Also check out community centers, college workout rooms, and your local YMCA or YWCA. Y's usually have workout facilities, and their memberships cost a lot less than those at health clubs. Plus, you don't have to pay extra for towels.

Do It Together

WORKING OUT TOGETHER is a great way to motivate and encourage each other, and to spend more time together. What about taking up a sport together, like hiking, tennis, rock climbing, golf, martial arts, yoga, or weight lifting? You can learn together, and enjoy the benefits of exercise along the way. You can also be there when frustration takes hold and temptation to quit kicks in. Single people have workout buddies, people they call to go to the gym or to play tennis. In fact, many report that knowing someone is waiting for them gets them to go. By taking up an activity together, you have an automatic incentive to get going. And when one partner gets discouraged, the other can be encouraging.

By blocking out some time to exercise together, you open up the opportunity to share something new and important in both of your lives, and build some hobbies and activities you can enjoy years into your marriage. Start small. Think of something you've always wanted to do but were afraid to try. Then, to quote a popular advertising slogan, just do it.

Resources

Anderson, Bob. *Stretching At Your Computer or Desk*. Bolinas, California: Shelter Publications, 1997.

Birch, Beryl Bender. *Power Yoga*. New York: Simon & Schuster, 1995.

Burke, Edmund R. *The Home Fitness Handbook*. Champaign, Illinois: Human Kinetics, 1996.

Francis, Peter, Ph.D., and Lorna Francis, Ph.D. *Real Exercise for Real People*. Rocklin, California: Prima Publishing, 1996.

SETTING AND ACHIEVING GOALS

The race is not to the swift nor the battle to the strong.
—Ecclesiastes 9:2

Much has been written about goals lately. You can hardly walk into a bookstore these days without being bombarded by books and audiotapes on achieving financial freedom, waking up giants, and prioritizing goals. Inspirational speakers fill mega-domes around the country, all because people are seeking a magic formula that can help them to achieve their goals.

Unfortunately, there are no magic solutions, no miracle processes that will work 100 percent of the time, contrary to what those all-smiles, exuberant, energetic, optimistic, well-groomed, pinky-ring-wearing slicksters would have you believe on late-night infomercials. The "If I can do it, you can" spiels may sound good, but by and large, the "everything-you-need-is-included" packages work for very few people. The "success stories" you see featured on infomercials—which, let's face it, is just a new word for long, annoying commercials—are paid actors. They have been made up to look like they're supposed to look, which is usually happy and wealthy, and they'll say whatever they get paid to say. Think about it. If they had really made $2 million last year, do you think they'd be appearing on a low-budget infomercial that advertises their income to the whole world? Not likely.

But I digress. Back to the subject at hand: goals. Everyone must have goals they are moving toward; otherwise, life becomes stagnant. For newlyweds, it's even more important to set and achieve goals if only because you will never be happy as a couple unless you're happy as individuals. And everyone knows that the way to happiness is meeting your goals, right?

Well, not exactly. The way to happiness begins with setting goals—that is, it begins with determining what will make you happy and then setting out to accomplish that. Your goal may be financial independence, or it may be having children. It may be finding a rewarding, challenging position at a creative, supportive company, or it may be buying a horse you can ride on the weekends. Whatever your picture of happiness, setting goals will get you there.

Setting goals helps you to organize your thoughts, create plans, solve problems, overcome obstacles, and move ahead. People who constantly set and achieve goals make more money, are more successful, are healthier, have stronger relationships, have less stress, have happier marriages, and are more confident than other people. These are the people who seem to be able to do anything and to have everything—they have the proverbial Midas touch.

Goals will win out over intelligence and talent almost every time. At least, persistence in trying to achieve goals will. If you start using goals right now, and track your progress in achieving them, your life will change so drastically in the next few years that you won't even recognize yourself. I guarantee it. Uh ... I mean, it is pretty likely.

But everyone has tried to achieve something, certainly, whether it was losing weight, making more money, getting a certain promotion. And everyone has failed at one time or another. There's nothing wrong with failing; it shows you're striving for something. The problem comes when people beat themselves up after a failure, engaging in negative and self-defeating thought patterns. They tell themselves, "I should have known I could never do that; next time I won't strive for something so far out of reach." And they don't try again.

Fear of failure is one of the most powerful deterrents to success. People simply don't think they can succeed. Hence, the popularity of books like *Awaken the Giant Within* by Anthony Robbins and audiotapes like *The Psychology of Achievement* by Brian Tracy. These publications and others like them first help people build up their confidence and overcome their fear of failure. Then they lay out organized, systematic methods for setting and achieving goals.

These systems are not universal: what works for some may not work for others. But establishing a system is an important first step in reaching a goal. And while luck may play a part in what happens to you, that part becomes less significant the more you organize and plan to meet your objectives.

When a goal isn't reached, it's not so much the person who has failed as it is his or her system. An unorganized, unplanned, hasty attempt to hit a target stands little chance of succeeding—you're unlikely to hit a bull's-eye if you're blindfolded and disoriented The following steps are an attempt to help you organize a methodical, logical plan of attack for setting and achieving your goals. For your convenience, sample journal pages are provided at the end of this chapter for each step.

Get Ready

1. **State your goal.** On the top of a notebook page—you may want to splurge on a seventy-nine-cent notebook for this one, or use the journal pages at the end of this chapter—write the word "Goal," and next to it exactly what it is that you intend to achieve.

Notice that I said "exactly" what you want to achieve. The way you state your goal is important: you have to be concrete and specific when you lay out your objective. Writing "I wish I could make more money" or "I want to be more organized" isn't going to help you chart a specific course of action for achieving your goal. On the other hand, writing "I will earn $5,000 more this year than last year" or "I will organize my office and my finances by the end of November" will get you started on the road to success.

Avoid stating your goal as a wish. When you wish for something, your mind hears, "that would be nice but I know I won't get it." A wish is something you hope for but don't really think is possible. Focus on what's possible, and say it like you mean it.

Thinking assertively is also important in stating goals. The human mind is a busy muscle. If you say, "Hey, Brain, sometime when you get around to it can you help me with this?" your brain will leave your goal waiting in line and filling out forms for weeks. If, on the other hand, you give your brain a well-defined "Now. Do it. Go," your goal can step right to the front of the line. It's a mental trick that positive thinkers have used for many years.

2. Set a deadline. Yeah, I know. You already have enough deadlines to live with, so why impose another on yourself? Well, if you're serious about achieving a goal, you must help your brain prioritize the information. Otherwise, you tend to tread water rather than moving ahead. For example, if you have no specific deadline for when you want to lose a certain amount of weight, your brain will allow you to cheat on your diet every once in a while because there's no hurry to lose the weight. ("If I eat this chocolate cream pie this weekend, I can work it off Monday morning before work.") When all is said and done, you end up losing the same ten pounds over and over and over and over and over again.

To set a deadline, divide the goal into doable chunks. If, for example, you weigh 265 pounds, your goal shouldn't be to weigh 190 pounds in a month. You need to set intermediate goals for the first five or ten pounds, then the next five or ten, and so on. Determine some reasonable intermediate goals for your main goal, and write them down in your notebook or on the journal pages at the back of this chapter.

Get Set

ONCE YOU HAVE established your goal, stated it in detail, and set a deadline, you're ready to load up the car to begin the journey.

3. Fill up your fuel tank. Start your journey with a full tank of gas. On your first Goal sheet, write down all the advantages of meeting your goal—why you want to achieve your goal and what you will enjoy once it is attained. List at least twenty things you will have, enjoy, or be able to do once you reach your goal. This is one of the most exciting steps in goal setting because it allows you to see all the benefits of reaching the goal laid out before you at once. The positive mental images you form by making this list will keep you going when you get discouraged. This is your fuel.

4. Locate your resources. Before you begin your journey, you need to determine what kind of help you will need to reach your objective. If your goal is to get a better job, for example, you'll need the help of the person who hires you. You'll also need information. Getting a better job may require learning who to contact, basic facts about the company, and how to go about getting your foot in the door. In locating your resources, consider a variety of sources—for instance, books, newsletters, trade magazines, the Internet, and so forth. Make a quick list of these resources to refer to while charting your course.

5. Anticipate obstacles. If you did not have obstacles to overcome, you'd have achieved your goal already. For this step, simply list those obstacles that may impede your progress or prevent you from accomplishing your objective. What is it that is stopping you or has stopped you in the past from achieving your goal?

Go

NOW, YOU'RE READY to act. Begin by making a plan.

6. Plan your route. Consolidate all the materials you've compiled to this point: You've set your destination, located available resources, and predicted your obstacles, now it's time to chart your course. Use your intermediate goal sheets to make one comprehensive "to do" list. On each intermediate goal sheet, list every step that is necessary to reach that next goal. When you've completed all your lists, you will have a comprehensive plan for achieving your overall goal.

For example, one intermediate goal of getting a better job might be to send out ten resumes a week to potential employers. Achieving that intermediate goal may require looking in the want ads, calling associates and professional contacts, visiting a personnel management office, going to the library to look at trade journals, even making cold calls to research information about certain companies. Another intermediate goal might be practicing mock interviews with colleagues, which could require reading information about proper interviewing techniques and scheduling time to practice.

Use your lists of resources and obstacles to help you plan your steps. If one of your obstacles is that the upcoming holiday weekend festivities will give you less time to send out ten resumes, for example, lay out a specific action that will help you overcome the obstacle—in this case, possibly making more networking calls the week before.

7. Just do it. No plan will work unless you put it into action. You've spent the time thinking it through, you've done your homework and know how to succeed. Now all you have to do is take each step on your list until you reach your goal.

8. Stay on track. It's important to review your plan every day until the goal is met, even if you've laid out intermediate steps for every other day. Look at your list. Add to it. Rewrite it. Focusing on your goal daily will keep everything clear in your head. For most people, the best time for this is first thing in the morning. When your mind is clear, concentrating even briefly on your goal will plant the thoughts in your mind of what needs to be done that day to reach your goal. And if you stick with it, reminding yourself of what needs to be done will get you moving.

You married your mate because you wanted to share your future together. Begin planning that future today. Set goals, locate resources, identify obstacles, chart your course, and stick with it. Before you know it, you'll be living your dream.

Resources

Robbins, Anthony. *Awaken the Giant Within*, New York: Fawcett, 1991.

Tracy, Brian. *The Psychology of Achievement*. Nightingale-Conant, 1984. Audiocassette.

Finley, Guy. *The Secret of Letting Go*. St. Paul: Llewellyn Publications, 1996.

JOURNAL PAGES

Goal

Intermediate Goal #1

Step 1

Step 2

Step 3

Step 4

Step 5

Step 6

Step 7

Intermediate Goal #2
Step 1

Step 2

Step 3

Step 4

Step 5

Step 6

Step 7

Intermediate Goal #3

Step 1

Step 2

Step 3

Step 4

Step 5

Step 6

Step 7

Intermediate Goal #4

Step 1

Step 2

Step 3

Step 4

Step 5

Step 6

Step 7

Intermediate Goal #5
Step 1

Step 2

Step 3

Step 4

Step 5

Step 6

Step 7

Intermediate Goal #6

Step 1

Step 2

Step 3

Step 4

Step 5

Step 6

Step 7

Resources

1.

2.

3.

4.

5.

6.

7.

Obstacles

1.

Counterplan:

2.

Counterplan:

3.

Counterplan:

4.

Counterplan:

5.

Counterplan:

6.

Counterplan:

7.

Counterplan:

HUH? WHAT'S THAT YOU SAY?

What we have here—is failure to communicate.
—the Warden to the inmates in Cool Hand Luke

When Debbie and I first started dating she would often begin a sentence with, "When you get a chance, would you mind …"

Of course, given my background and gender, I processed that to mean, "When you get a chance, would you mind . . ." But what it really meant, or so I have been repeatedly told, was, "Within the next ten minutes do this for me, because if it's not done in fifteen minutes I'll do it myself and assume that you had absolutely no intention of doing it in the first place."

I didn't understand her. Plain and simple. When we wed, I assumed she spoke English and meant what she said. But she doesn't, I don't—none of us do. We all send underlying messages, make weird interpretations, and have strange expectations. Newlyweds, however, have it worse, for they are in love. They think their partners will be able to go beyond the spoken word, to know what they're thinking and feeling and wanting. When they say, "Open the window," they expect their spouses to know that what they really want them to do is go and get them a milkshake. After all, their mates know them better than anyone on earth. As it should be. Trouble is, no one knows you that well.

The following is a short translation dictionary I've put together from my own experiences and those of my seminar students. Feel free to add your own to the list; more than likely, you'll have plenty to add in just a few months. That's the beauty of the English language—lots of room for translation.

Spoken Word	Translation
Honey, do we have any plans this weekend?	You are going to have plans for the weekend in five seconds.
Where's the remote?	Stop switching back and forth between stations.
Did you have to work late?	Where the hell have you been?
Are you ready?	Let's go already!
Does this make me look fat?	Tell me I'm beautiful/handsome.
Do you think she's pretty?	Why are you looking at her instead of me?
Do you think he's good-looking?	What's so great about him? What's he got that I don't?
Do you mind if I go out?	Look, I'm smiling. That means I still love you, so let me go. OK? Please oh please oh please.
I have a headache.	Dream on.
There's nothing else on.	Sit back and relax. You're in for a treat. *Blood Orgy of the Amazon*—it's a classic.
I love it when you …	Do that or something like it again, and often.
Do you like this recipe?	If you don't eat it, I'm not going to cook for you again.
I can't move.	It's your turn to take out the garbage.
You don't have to get me anything this year.	… and I want a new set of skis and a new coat and those boots I saw and a new CD player …

Everything became clearer when, after about a year of marriage, my brain was fitted with a Debbie-Jean Universal Translator. Up until then, she'd ask for a fork and I'd bring her the car jack. The same will probably be true for you. A year into your marriage, you will know your partner in a deeper way than you ever thought possible. You will be able to read your mate's mind and know what he or she wants, sometimes before or better than your mate does. And each year your relationship will grow stronger and stronger until you'll hardly be able to believe the strength of the bond you've constructed. That's what marriage is all about.

Well, all right, not always. But if this scenario doesn't exactly characterize your marriage, don't fret. The fact of the matter is, marriages come in all shapes and sizes, just like people and fish. What's more, marriages change over time, as people do. You married your spouse, hopefully, because you could envision spending the rest of your life with that person. You wanted to be closer to your wife than to anyone else. You wanted your husband to know you better than anyone ever has. You signed on to share your lives, and you now must find a way to make those lives one.

Never Stop Talking

LIFE IS experience. Knowledge comes from experience. Sometimes that knowledge is hard fought; other times it drops in your lap. Wisdom and personal growth come from processing knowledge, which is stimulated by communication. If you're lucky, you and your new mate will share many years of dreams and laughter. How closely you share those years is entirely up to you.

Successful marriages, like all relationships, require talking, talking, and more talking. Communication is the key to finding mutual ground during disputes and higher ground after the axe has fallen. As the old saying goes, "As long as you're still talking...."

Oh, and by the way, congratulations. On your marriage, or on your engagement, and on your new life together. Make it a good one.

INDEX